Soccer Goalkeeping
The Last Line of Defense
The First Line of Attack

Lincoln Phillips

MASTERS PRESS

NTC/Contemporary Publishing Group

Library of Congress Cataloging-in-Publication Data

Phillips, Lincoln.
    Soccer goalkeeping : the last line of defense, the first line of attack / Lincoln
Phillips.
       p.   cm.
    ISBN 1-57028-077-0
    1. Soccer—Goalkeeping.   I. Title.   II. Series.
GV943.9.G62P55   1995
796.334'26—dc20   95-50988
                                                   CIP

Cover design by Suzanne Lincoln
Artwork by Scott Stadler

Published by Masters Press
A division of NTC/Contemporary Publishing Group, Inc.
4255 West Touhy Avenue, Lincolnwood (Chicago), Illinois 60712-1975 U.S.A.
Copyright © 1996 by Lincoln Phillips
Printed in the United States of America
International Standard Book Number: 1-57028-077-0

00 01 02 03 04 05 RCP 21 20 19 18 17 16 15 14 13 12 11 10 9 8 7 6 5 4

Preface

A goalkeeper must be a reliable stronghold as the last defender. His solid performance inspires the activities of his teammates, their determination and the confidence in attack and defense. He operates in a crowded area where offensive and defensive efforts are clashing decisively, arousing the peak of tension and excitement. His anticipation of the opponents' attacking maneuvers from the outset to the final stages, and his rapid adjustment to apply his skills with coolness and composure are the significant attributes of his performance.

All activities of a soccer player are in the first place mental processes. The goalkeeper will enhance his perception, his decision and action ability, by reading and responding to realistic and dynamic match situations. From the very beginning in the functional training routine, a goalkeeper will frequently react to teammates releasing simple passes or shots determined by the coach. The goalkeeper learns to adjust himself to catch or parry shots from various angles and distances demanding all the basic skills, one by one.

The quality goalkeeper is an example of total dedication, concentration and self-discipline. He never surrenders and will always look ahead to master the next challenge.

Lincoln Phillips, the author of this manual on goalkeeping, played the position himself at the international and peak professional levels. His philosophy and approach to developing the goalkeeper's performance from the beginner to the professional is based upon his own practical experience and thorough evaluation. In applying and constantly refining this philosophy as a coach at the state, national and professional levels, Lincoln is the most competent to convey his knowledge as a valuable aid to coaches and players alike.

I hope that many coaches and players will seize the chance to benefit from Lincoln's experience and advice.

Karl-Heinz Heddergott

Former Director of Coaching, Federal Republic of Germany
Staff Coach, F.I.F.A.
Former Director of Coaching, United States Soccer Federation

Credits:
_____
Cover design: Suzanne Lincoln
Artwork: Scott Stadler

Acknowledgments

This book is written for *everyone* interested in the art of goalkeeping. It is intended to be useful to players, coaches, and others who might wish to equip themselves with a better understanding of goalkeeping.

Throughout this book, players are referred to with masculine pronouns — I say *he* instead of *she* or *he/she*. That is not to imply that females do not make great goalkeepers. On the contrary, females are excellent goalkeepers, and I am thrilled to see soccer cross gender lines. I expressed this concern to my editor at Masters Press, and she assured me that in standard English *he* is a generic pronoun and not meant to be exclusive. I hope the use of *he* throughout this book does not deter any young girl's enthusiasm for soccer. I welcome women of all ages to this wonderful sport.

I am grateful beyond words to David Nesbitt for his encouragement, insights, critiques and exhaustive editing in the early stages of the manuscript. I express particular thanks to Linda Powell for her extraordinary skill and patience in editing the manuscript in its latter stages. I am also grateful to Richard Shea for his editorial assistance and encouragement at a time when I thought I would never complete this book. Special thanks to my dear friend Anthony Campbell who made his secretary, Debbie Gaspard, available to type and edit this book.

Karl-Heinz Heddergott has given me and this project tremendous support. I am especially grateful that he has written the foreword to this book in his capacity as F.I.F.A. Staff Coach. Likewise, I am grateful to Alan Hodgkinson for writing a foreword in his capacity of Goalkeeping Coach for the Scottish Football Association.

I acknowledge my obligation to Malcolm Cook, Director of Youth Development, Liverpool F.C.; Bernd Shunk, Assistant Coach, F.C. Cologne; Victor Gamaldo, undoubtedly the best defender I have ever played with; Ian Bain, Head Coach, Washington Diplomats; and Tony DiCicco, Director, Soccer Plus Goalkeeping Schools. Their encouragement, critiques and suggestions were of inestimable value. I am indebted to John Liparini and Hugh Cole of Brantly Development Corporation, First American Bank of Washington, D.C., and The Columbia Bank for their financial support.

Thanks to Diana Mardall who carefully shepherded the manuscript's multiple revisions through the word processor. I also wish to thank Blondelle Hunter, Martha Sears and Carrie Bennett for their assistance in typing some early drafts.

This book owes much to its illustrations. I wish to thank Linda Powell who took most of the pictures. Debbie Sommers, Tony Quinn, Louise Waxler and Stephen Slade were extremely helpful in shooting some of the pictures, especially at short notice. I am also indebted to Teddy Gregor for the fine work he did on the drawing concepts.

Five players participated in the demonstrations — Nick Broujos, Steve Powers, Jim Kelly, Manny Sanchez, Thom Skoglund, Russell Payne and Richard Avis. I wish to thank them for their dedication, enthusiasm and patience during the long photo sessions.

I wish to express my deepest gratitude to my mother and father for all the support and encouragement they provided me. Also to my sisters and brothers, Alicia, Marilyn, Wilbert, Georgie, Winston and Euan. The following individuals played a vital role in shaping my philosophy and pushing my thinking in new directions: Kelvin "Pa" Aleong, Conrad Braithwaite, Geoff Chambers, Desmond Whiskey, Geoff Serrette, Carlton Dore, Robert Farrell, Egbert Pierre, Rex Duhurst, Horace Springer, the late Dr. Hermon Tyrance, Ted Chambers, Dr. Marshall Banks, Dr. Carl Anderson, Milton Miles, Al Collins, Clive Toye, Eugene Ringsdorf and Kelvin Joseph.

I am eternally grateful to the goalkeepers who contributed significantly to shaping my philosophy and style in goalkeeping — Hugh Sealy, whose flamboyant style of goalkeeping I imitated right down to his all-black attire; Joey Gonsalves, Cax Baptiste, Pat Gomez and Clive Burnett were my mentors; Lev Yashin of Russia; Gordon Banks, Bob Wilson and Peter Bonetti of England; and Carmelo of Spain provided me with a postgraduate education in the art of goalkeeping.

I am deeply indebted to all the club and school teams for giving me the opportunity to represent them — St. Crispin's E.C. School, Wanderers F.C., Spartak F.C., Queen's Royal College, Providence F.C., Maple F.C. Regiment, The Trinidad-Tobago National Team, Baltimore Bays, Washington Darts, and Baltimore Comets. I am particularly grateful to all my teammates, especially the defensive players who were so instrumental in my success as a goalkeeper. I am also grateful for the opportunity of coaching in the following leagues and associations: North American Soccer League, United States Soccer Federation, Maryland State Youth Soccer Association, Soccer Association of Columbia, Montgomery Soccer Incorporated and Seneca Soccer Association. The experiences I gathered through the various clinics and coaching courses were invaluable in helping me to write this book.

For the last six years, my wife, Linda, has seen, typed and listened to more drafts of this book than anyone can imagine. I deeply appreciate her understanding, patience, and constant encouragement. Without her support this book would not have been published. I am also grateful to my sons, Sheldon, Sean, Greg and Derek for just being great kids.

Lincoln Phillips

Foreword

Most successful teams I know and, indeed, those championship teams on the professional and World Cup levels, all possess similar qualities - one of which is consistency in the goalkeeping position. The quality goalkeeper will therefore win championships.

In spite of the growing awareness of the relationship between quality goalkeeping and championship teams, it really astounds me how little advice goalkeepers receive and the insufficient amount of information that is available on this topic.

When I first read Lincoln's book on goalkeeping, the title immediately caught my eye: *Goalkeeping: The Last Line of Defense: The First Line Of Attack*. The title alone implied that a more in-depth study of the art of goalkeeping was expected in the forthcoming chapters than the usual superficial treatment allotted to goalkeeping in many books. Lincoln has taken the goalkeeping position and broken it down into its simplest form so that young goalkeepers and their coaches can benefit from it. He has built the position from its simplest form to the most complex stage so that even the top professional goalkeeper could identify. Lincoln has played the goalkeeping position on the First Division and professional levels. He has had the opportunity to face some of the world's most outstanding strikers, including Pele, George Eastham, Terry Venables, Ade Coker, and Clyde Best. His work not only reflects his experience as a top level goalkeeper but also as an outfield player and professional coach.

As a professional goalkeeper coach I have had the opportunity to coach some of the best goalkeepers in the world, including Peter Shilton, Neville Southall, Pat Bonner, and Tim Leighton, along with numerous apprentice professionals and youth goalkeepers. I am, therefore, always on the alert for any information articles, books or videotapes — that will supplement my teachings. I give Lincoln's book a four star rating. This is the highest compliment I can give because this book gives me, after 23 years of professional playing and coaching, the information I need to share with the professional goalkeepers of today as well as the aspiring professional goalkeepers of tomorrow.

I recommend *Soccer Goalkeeping: The Last Line of Defense, The First Line of Attack* to anyone who is interested in the art of goalkeeping.

Alan Hodgkinson

Former English National Team Goalkeeper (1957 — 1961)
Professional Goalkeeper Coach
Scottish Football Association

Contents

Part Two: Goalkeeping Technique.........2?

This book is dedicated to
my wife Linda,
my sons Sheldon, Sean, Greg and Derek
and to
my parents, brothers and sisters.

Understanding The Goalkeeper's Role

In soccer the goalkeeper is the captain of the team's defense. No other player has as many responsibilities bestowed upon him. The goalkeeper is expected to utilize his skills in defending his goal. When he is in possession of the ball, he is expected to initiate an attack with every clearance. He must also possess the ability to read and understand the game in order to communicate effectively with his teammates. The goalkeeper is one of the most important players on the field, if not the most important player.

What baffles me most of all is the treatment most goalkeepers — even on the professional level — receive compared to their outfield teammates. They are treated like the poor relations in a family — pushed off to some remote corner of the practice field to fend for themselves and summoned only when it is in the best interest of the outfield players — shooting practice. I do not know of any other sport where the players who play in the most important positions are neglected.

Another bitter pill to swallow is the misconceived notion among coaches that all goalkeepers are a bit crazy. As a former goalkeeper, I personally resent that notion. I have met and played against some of the best goalkeepers in the world and never detected craziness as a common denominator among them. I have met many a crazy forward, halfback, defender and goalkeeper in my time. But craziness is not a prerequisite for goalkeeping.

Only when coaches become more knowledgeable about the importance of goalkeeping, goalkeeping skills and the psychological dimension of goalkeeping can these problems be erased. This section is designed to assist the reader in getting a better understanding of goalkeeping.

Chapter 1

The Importance of Goalkeeping

The success of World Cup and national champions is often attributed to the deployment of key players in strategic positions. These key positions include central striker, central halfback, central defenders, and most important, the goalkeeper.

To reduce the game of soccer to its simplest terms, a team's prime objectives are (1) to score goals and (2) to prevent opponents' scoring. Thus, a brilliant save by the goalkeeper becomes every bit as important to a team's success as a brilliant shot on the other end of the field. It sometimes baffles me how little attention goalkeepers receive compared to their outfield teammates. Yet, during a game, handling difficult shots cleanly or diving courageously toward an attacker's feet can be inspiring, instilling enough confidence in teammates that they perform well above their heads. Opponents, on the other hand, become very discouraged seeing their best efforts thwarted by the goalkeeper.

A quality goalkeeper can very well cause the opposing team to doubt their shooting ability or chances of scoring, causing them to either seek scoring chances closer to the goal, shoot inaccurately out of frustration, or cease shooting altogether. Conversely, a goalkeeper who appears shaky can produce the opposite effect; defenders will soon lose confidence in him while opponents will seize every opportunity to shoot. (How many times have you heard coaches urge their players to shoot more often because the goalkeeper looks shaky?)

Shot stopping, however, is merely one aspect of efficient goalkeeping, and it is merely one result of the integration of several critical roles every goalkeeper must play. Each of these roles will be discussed in detail later in this book. However, from a general point of view, in addition to being (1) a defender (shot stopping) and (2) an attacker (distribution), a goalkeeper must also perform the roles of (3) an observer and communicator; and (4) a tactician.

The Goalkeeper as Defender

The goalkeeper is the last line of defense. When all else fails to stem an attack, the burden of preventing the score ultimately falls on the goalkeeper.

As the last defender, the goalkeeper's main function is protecting the goal from shots arriving at tremendous speeds, from varying angles, and, at times, from point-blank range. In no other position does any one player have as many decisions to make, in such a short time, as the goalkeeper. Forwards and defenders make mistakes (many of which go unnoticed), but when the goalkeeper errs, it is usually fatal: a goal. I have seen goalkeepers perform brilliantly for 89 minutes, then make one mistake during the last 60 seconds and cause their team to lose.

As a defender, the goalkeeper is in a decisive position. Concentration throughout the game is essential. The goalkeeper must attempt to catch the ball cleanly with one touch, or deflect uncatchable shots high or wide of the goal. "Safety first" should be every goalkeeper's motto.

In many ways the goalkeeper plays a role similar to that of a sweeper. He must follow the game closely (even when the ball is at the other end of the field), and take care to maintain a proper position in relation to the position of the ball and the rear-most defender. For example, by applying the defensive principle of compactness (Fig. 1-1A-C), the goalkeeper must adjust his position to that of his last defender. Thus, the entire penalty area may and should be used. Moreover, the goalkeeper should never hesitate to venture outside of the penalty area if the game situation demands. The distance ventured outside the penalty area would depend on the physical attributes of the goal-keeper — speed, agility, height etc.

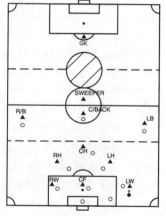 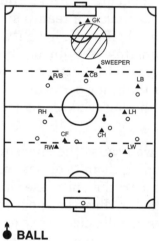 

BALL

Figure 1-1A: *The attacking team ▲ has advanced the ball in the attacking 1/3 of the field. The goalkeeper supports the space behind ⬯ the sweeper.*

Figure 1-1B: *The ▲ loses possession of the ball and the attacker O's are in possession. The ball is advanced into the ▲'s middle 1/3 of the field. As the ▲'s sweeper drops back, so does the goalkeeper.*

Figure 1-1C: *O's are now in a dangerous position just outside ▲'s penalty area. The goalkeeper again adjust his position to cover the space behind the sweeper and also to protect his goal from attacks.*

The Goalkeeper as Observer and Communicator

The goalkeeper is in the best position to observe all 21 remaining players from an angle of 180 degrees. He is able to see teammates push forward in attack and fall back in defense; when defenders are out of position (i.e. too far to one side of the field, too high up the field or too far back) or are not tracking down players. From this strategic position, the goalkeeper can play an extremely vital role as an observer.

However, seeing attacking and defensive maneuvers as they unfold is meaningless unless the goalkeeper has the knowledge and experience to interpret what he sees.

Furthermore, he must possess the ability to communicate those observations effectively to the defenders. When the goalkeeper instructs teammates, the words must be loud, clear, and easily understood — for example "Keeper!", "Man on!", "Move out!", "Turn!", "Behind you!" At the same time, however, the goalkeeper must be careful that loud non-informational shouting is not mistaken for purposeful comment.

Many defenders readily admit how helpful it is to have an experienced goalkeeper passing on useful information to them during the course of the game. The goalkeeper acts as "the eyes behind the defenders' heads."

A quick word from the goalkeeper can plug up dangerous gaps in the defense, often reducing the number of opportunities for shots on goal. The goalkeeper can also help motivate his teammates to a higher level of performance by acknowledging outstanding individual efforts during the course of the game.

The Goalkeeper as Tactician

A goalkeeper must be knowledgeable about the game in order to be effective in directing its course. For example, if a free kick is awarded for the opponents just outside the penalty area, the goalkeeper's instructions to form a wall must be quick and command his teammates' attention: "Barrier!" or "Wall!", "Five players!" (in the wall), or "Six players!" as the case may be.

The goalkeeper must also possess the tactical ability to control the tempo of the game when the ball is in his possession, slowing things down or speeding the game up with quick counterattacks. For example, suppose that his team's defense has been under pressure for a long period, causing his teammates up front to drop back on defense. Upon regaining possession of the ball, the goalkeeper should elect to slow the game down and allow his attacking teammates time to move back into the front line. Conversely, a goalkeeper who sees an opportunity to make a quick outlet pass to a fullback or halfback, or a long penetrative pass to the back of the opponents' defense for an attacking teammate, should elect to speed the game up.

Modern soccer dictates that, on loss of possession, each player becomes a defender and is bound by the principles of defense. On the other hand, when a team regains possession of the ball, all players are bound by the principles of attack. The goalkeeper is not exempt from any of these defensive or attacking principles. Quality goalkeepers must possess the technical skill necessary to distribute the ball accurately and the tactical ability to know when and where to distribute so that they initiate attacking movements with every distribution. They must decide whether it is in the best interest of their team to throw or to kick the ball. They must endeavor to release accurate passes kicked or thrown to unmarked teammates or into spaces where teammates have a good chance of winning the ball. They must also consider the quality of every distribution, so that each pass provides the greatest opportunity for teammates to retain possession of the ball.

I have observed many goalkeepers who are able to kick the ball powerfully, but who consistently admire the distance of their own punts with no thought as to how the kick has wasted a creative opportunity. Many goalkeepers do not realize that the greater the number of 50/50 balls put into play, the greater the risk of increasing their own workload.

This chapter has touched briefly on the roles and the importance of the goalkeeper. These will be explained in detail in later chapters, but the first step in creating a solid, well rounded team begins with a solid understanding of these most basic aspects.

Chapter 2

Essential Requirements For A Quality Goalkeeper

Although many coaches faced with the task of selecting a goalkeeper favor a tall, agile athlete, many great goalkeepers have been short and slightly built. Regardless of their physical characteristics, however, quality goalkeepers possess certain common attributes. This chapter will outline what I consider to be the essential requirements for a quality goalkeeper.

Height

At the high school, college, and professional levels, the ideal height for a goalkeeper ranges from 5'11" to 6'3". All other things being equal, tall goalkeepers have certain advantages over their shorter counterparts. For example, a short goalkeeper will be forced to turn more shots over the crossbar or around the uprights — thus conceding more corner kicks than a taller goalkeeper who, because of his extra reach, might be in a better position to catch the ball cleanly. However, coaches should not select taller goalkeepers with poor catching technique over shorter ones who possess sound technique, good jumping ability, and good timing.

Coaches, especially on the youth level, should never discourage any player from being, or attempting to be, a goalkeeper on the basis of height or body size. There are qualities other than height that make a good goalkeeper.

Physical Fitness

It is foolish to believe that, because the goalkeeper covers only a small area of the field, he need not be physically fit. This notion is utterly false. The nature of goalkeeping demands a high degree of all-round physical fitness.

The components of physical fitness are: strength, agility, flexibility, speed and endurance.

Strength

Strength is the ability to express force against resistance. It affects performance efficiency. Thus, for a goalkeeper, the explosive actions of sprinting, sudden stopping, jumping, diving, throwing, and kicking all require strength (explosive power). Strength is also necessary to prevail in situations around the penalty area that involve physical contact.

Agility and Flexibility

Both agility and flexibility are vital to quality goalkeeping. Agility is ease of physical reaction to unpredictable motor challenges. Flexibility is suppleness in performing a wide range of movements. For example, visualize a game situation in which an attacker gets off a powerful shot on a wet field with several players (attackers and defenders) obstructing the goalkeeper's view. The goalkeeper starts moving to the left in an effort to get behind the flight of the ball, only to see the shot deflect off a player's leg and ricochet in the opposite direction. The goalkeeper's ability to react to this effectively will depend largely upon agility and flexibility.

A goalkeeper's agility and flexibility will also allow him to:

• react decisively to point-blank shots.

• deal effectively with ricochets and obstructed view situations.

• change direction (while his feet are grounded or in the air) and throw his body into position to block shots.

• dive to the ground to make a save and be back on his feet in a flash to make another save or two (reloading).

Speed

Speed can be defined as the capacity to move the body at the greatest velocity. As it relates to goalkeeping, speed can be considered at two levels: *acceleration* (speed off the mark), and *quickness of thought and reaction* (perception-action).

Acceleration (speed off the mark from a standing start) is essential in moving the goalkeeper's body weight across the face of the goal and off the goal line to cut off crosses or through passes. In these three instances the goalkeeper must get off the mark very quickly to deprive oncoming attackers (who are sometimes closer to the ball) of shots on goal.

Quickness of thought and reaction is another absolute necessity for the goalkeeper who might be called upon to save shots at point-blank range. The goalkeeper must decide, within a fraction of a second, whether to dive for the ball or stay upright; to move off the goal line to intercept a high cross or stay "home," or if it is in the team's best interest to kick or throw the ball.

In order to do his job effectively, the goalkeeper must possess not only a wide array of technical skills but also the ability to select and utilize the most appropriate of these skills on the spur of the moment. Both sensitivity to relevant cues from an oncoming attacker and technical ability to respond accurately will influence the goalkeeper's speed of movement in any situation that requires quick reaction.

Endurance

The ability to withstand fatigue is absolutely essential in goalkeeping. Fatigue affects concentration. Lack of concentration leads to errors.

As mentioned in Chapter 1, the goalkeeper must provide compactness for the team by supporting the space behind the last defender. That space encompasses every bit of the penalty area and sometimes 10 to 15 yards or more outside the penalty area. During a game the goalkeeper might be called on to sprint forward to intercept a through pass, then immediately jump to catch or deflect a series of crossballs. Before he recovers, he may be forced to dive a few times to deflect shots over the crossbar or around the uprights. All of these movements, if done under pressure and for an extended period of time (5-10 minutes), require stamina. It is important, however, that the goalkeeper's endurance training be specific to his position. Requiring the goalkeeper to do the same type of endurance training as the outfield players is counterproductive.

Mental and Psychological Attributes

The goalkeeper, more than any other player, requires a high degree of mental toughness. His wide range of tasks, sometimes under dangerous circumstances, coupled with the continuing burden of being the last defender, can make the mental game as difficult as it is crucial.

Following are some of the mental attributes I consider to be vital to a goalkeeper (See Chapter 15 — The Psychological Dimension of Goalkeeping).

Concentration

Lack of concentration is one of the main reasons why goalkeepers make mistakes. Concentration is the ability to follow the ebb and flow of play for the entire duration of the game. The goalkeeper must be aware of the game and position himself in relation to the position of the ball and the rear-most defender. This principle holds true even if the ball is in front of his goal or at the opposite end of the field. The goalkeeper must be mentally alert in order to anticipate frequent changes in possession of the ball and be prepared to react decisively when called upon. Goals will be scored in almost every soccer game, and the goalkeeper must not allow such a setback to affect concentration. I have seen many talented goalkeepers who, when their teams are ahead, perform like world-beaters. But whenever their teams conceded a goal, their performance becomes mediocre at best, with the goalkeeper dropping balls because he is either thinking of the goal scored earlier or trying too hard in an effort to compensate for past mistakes.

Confidence

Confidence comes from knowing that you are well prepared. Only when a goalkeeper, after working conscientiously in practice, has achieved a high level of technical and tactical awareness can he feel truly confident.

A confident goalkeeper is convinced that he is able to deal effectively with any game situation. Sometimes he is even anxious for the attackers to get off a few good shots so he can get some action. On the other hand, if a goalkeeper knows that he is having problems judging high crosses or handling low shots cleanly, he is likely to become uneasy and lose confidence when these situations occur.

Generally, when a goalkeeper lacks confidence, it is due mainly to technical deficiencies, inability to read the game, or both.

Courage

The goalkeeper must possess enough mental toughness and competitive spirit to be willing to venture into dangerous situations; for example, to come off the line to punch a high crossball away from oncoming attackers. He knows that coming off the line to punch the ball is the correct decision, but he is also aware of the physical punishment that is sure to follow after colliding with the onrushing attacker. Making the decision to go for the ball in spite of the impending danger is the sign of a courageous player.

Competitiveness is the cornerstone of a courageous performance.

Composure

Composure is best described as the goalkeeper's ability to remain calm and maintain his poise especially after conceding a goal, when facing dangerous situations, or when provoked either through verbal abuse from opponents or teammates, or physical attacks by overanxious forwards.

The quality goalkeeper is the one who can maintain composure throughout the game — who is at ease in any situation. The more intense the situation, the calmer such a goalkeeper becomes, and the more he raises his own level of play.

Technical Proficiency

A major part of the goalkeeper's time is devoted to ball handling — catching, receiving low and waist high shots, punching, diving, etc. A quality goalkeeper must be proficient in all the technical aspects of ball handling. Technique is the cornerstone to a skillful performance.

Understanding of the Game

The goalkeeper is in a very strategic position between the uprights, able to see the entire field and all 21 players from an angle of 180 degrees. From this vantage point, the goalkeeper can observe rapid changes in the game as they evolve and must be prepared to act accordingly by either initiating defensive maneuvers (i.e. coming off the goal line to intercept a through pass or crossball) or passing on information to teammates so they can individually or collectively prevent the opponents' attack on goal.

In order to execute these functions effectively, the goalkeeper must be able to read and understand the game. He must understand the principles of attack and defense; the function of each player (especially his defenders); the laws of the game; and the various attacking maneuvers he is likely to face.

Charles Hughes writes in his book, *Tactics and Teamwork*, that the goalkeeper who can read and understand the game will be able "to anticipate immediate and future developments which will ultimately assist him in making correct decisions." The goalkeeper who is deficient in this aspect of the game "cannot play an authoritative part in the widest sense, in directing its course."

Consistency

Consistency is the ingredient that separates quality goalkeepers from average ones. Goalkeepers must always strive for consistent performances by being alert at all times in order to anticipate and react to dangerous situations, catching balls cleanly, and making sound decisions.

There are times when goalkeepers lose games solely on their own through technical errors, late movement off the goal line, or misjudging a high cross. According to Alan Hodgkinson an average goalkeeper is one who single-handedly loses a game on his own by giving up a goal one of every five games. A good goalkeeper loses one of every ten games, and a quality goalkeeper loses one of every twenty. Thus, the quality goalkeeper will win championships. Consistency is the hallmark of outstanding goalkeeping.

Chapter 3

Identifying Goalkeepers At The Youth Level

This chapter is directed to the many youth coaches who have the unenviable task of selecting players for the goalkeeping position. Usually when the question of who wants to be goalkeeper arises, hardly anyone volunteers and the coach must eventually select some reluctant youngster.

There are several reasons why young players prefer to play in outfield positions. They have boundless energy and prefer positions that allow them to run about and "have fun." They view goalkeeping as a dull position with little or no action. Second, the goalkeeper takes all the blame when a goal is scored. There is tremendous pressure from teammates and, very often, from the coach. Other players can make mistakes and get away with them, but when a goalkeeper errs, he is singled out as the person responsible for losing the game. Most children, naturally, do not like that kind of pressure, and their parents like it even less. Consequently, many parents ask the coach to play their child in any position other than goalkeeper. I know of parents who have actually threatened to take their children off of teams if the coach played them in goal. Third, there is a shortage of coaches with sufficient knowledge to teach youth players. As a result, goalkeepers receive little or no attention and very little constructive advice. Only when coaches view goalkeeping as an important position, indeed vital to the success of any team, can the negative attitude of young players toward goalkeeping be altered.

The following hints and suggestions are designed to help coaches identify young players with good goalkeeping potential:

Look For Athletes Who Excel In Relevant Skills From Other Sports

Basketball

1. good catching ability
2. excellent rebounding, combining strength with positioning and explosive jumping ability
3. the ability to cut off passes and steal balls through anticipation, speed, agility, quick reflexes, and aggressiveness
4. good ball handling skills, e.g. dribbling, passing, and shooting with either hand
5. the ability to control the tempo of the game, e.g. point guard
6. leadership qualities — emotional control, helping others remain cool in tense situations

Football (American)

1. (defensive backs and wide receivers) — good catching ability, speed (quick feet), strength, flexibility and quick reflexes
2. (offensive and defensive linemen) — good explosive power in getting off the mark and jumping, courage in taking on opponents and having no fear of making contact with opponents or the ground

Volleyball

1. good leaping ability (in blocking and spiking)
2. sharp reflexes (in recovering spikes)

Baseball

1. good catching and fielding abilities (catchers, first basemen and shortstops are prime prospects)

Cricket

1. good catching ability (wicketkeepers)
2. sharp reflexes and good hands in fielding positions close to the batsman

If a coach is observant and cognizant of goalkeeping skills, he can easily identify good goalkeeping prospects in other sports. However, a coach who assumes control of a team with no prior knowledge of individual players' strengths and weaknesses will have to start from scratch in selecting the best or most suitable player for each position on the field.

Use Specialized Exercises to Help Identify the Best Goalkeeping Prospects.

I would suggest the following games:

Throw and catch game

The game is played on a 20 X 40 yard field with two goals at each end (Fig. 3-1), approximately 3-4 yards wide. Two teams compete to see which one scores the most goals. The game is similar to basketball except for a few variations. The players spread out and attempt to pass the ball to their teammates. When the ball is caught the player in possession can only run a maximum of 3-4 steps, then another pass must be made.

Method of scoring: a goal can only be scored by a header.

In Figure 3-1 the attacking player A makes a pass chest high to his teammate B who catches the ball and runs to B1. At this point B1 then delivers an overarm pass to C who jumps high above the opponents to catch the ball. Player C runs to C1 and makes a pass to the feet of his teammate D. Player D collects the low pass and runs to D1 making a lofted pass for his teammate E to score on a header.

Throw-Head-Catch Game

This game is similar to the one in Figure 3-1 with one exception: the ball must be headed after it is thrown. In Figure 3-2 the attacking player A throws a pass to his

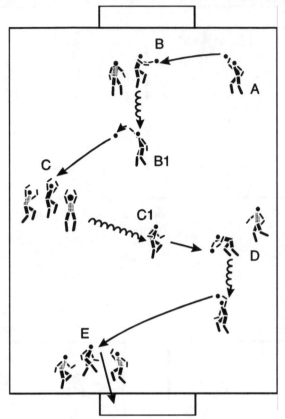

Figure 3-1

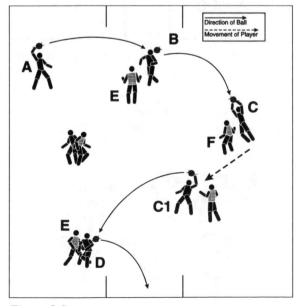

Figure 3-2

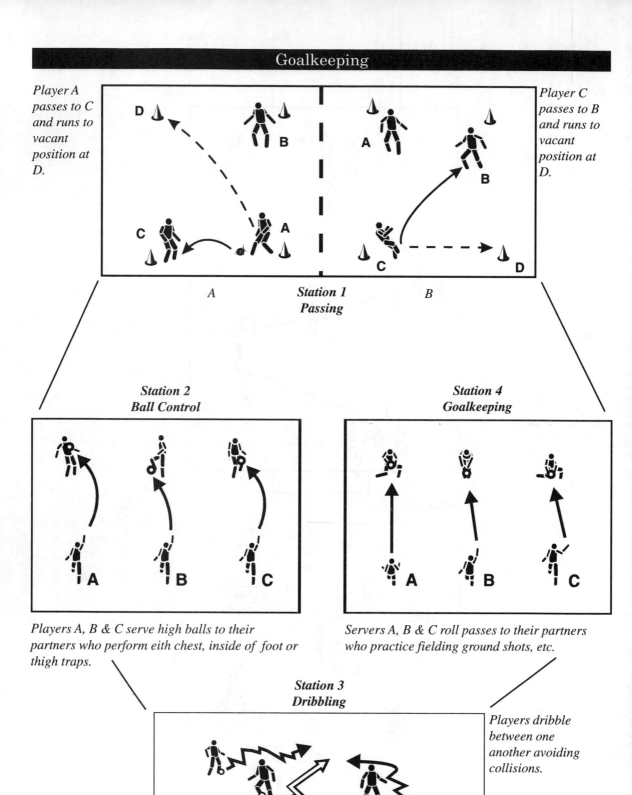

Player A passes to C and runs to vacant position at D.

Player C passes to B and runs to vacant position at D.

A

B

Station 1
Passing

Station 2
Ball Control

Players A, B & C serve high balls to their partners who perform eith chest, inside of foot or thigh traps.

Station 4
Goalkeeping

Servers A, B & C roll passes to their partners who practice fielding ground shots, etc.

Station 3
Dribbling

Players dribble between one another avoiding collisions.

Figure 3-3

18

teammate B. At this point the ball must be played with the head of either defender E or attacking player B. Player B heads the ball to his teammate C who jumps high in the air to catch the ball. Player C runs a few steps to C1 and throws a pass to his teammate D who scores with a header.

These two games are ideal for warm-ups. Players not only move around the field constantly, but also are involved in throwing, catching, jumping (goalkeeping skills) and heading. Natural goalkeeping prospects will stand out in these games

Circuit Training

Set up three to four stations with a different technique to be practiced at each station (e.g. passing, ball control, dribbling, goalkeeping). Organize groups of four to six players. Each group will practice for 5 to 10 minutes at one station, then rotate in a clockwise direction to a new station until each group gets the opportunity to practice every technique (Fig. 3-3). The following drills are suggested for the goalkeeping station: in 2's or 3's, players are taught the fundamentals of receiving low shots, catching and diving.

Shooting Drills

Use cones to mark a goal for each group of three players involved in the shooting drill (Fig. 3-4). In Figure 3-4A, player A serves as the goalkeeper. Player B is stationed with the ball approximately 10 to 20 yards (depending on the age of the children) from the goal. Player C stands 10-20 yards out, opposite B. The drill begins when B shoots on goal, following up the shot in case the goalkeeper does not field the ball cleanly. After the shot the ball goes to C, (Fig. 3-4B) who becomes the shooter. Player B will then

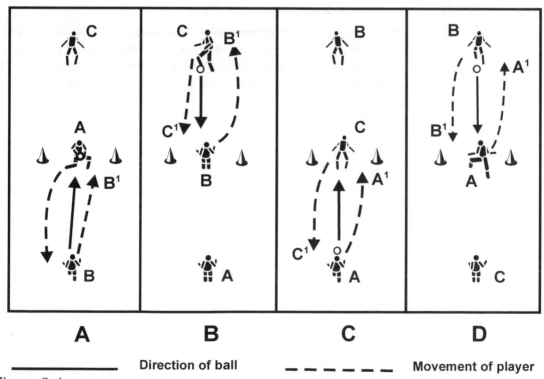

A	B	C	D

————————— **Direction of ball**   — — — — — — **Movement of player**

Figure 3-4

19

change places with A and become the goalkeeper. Player A moves behind the goal. The same sequence is repeated, with the shooter moving into the goal, the goalkeeper replacing the shooter, and the third player getting an opportunity to shoot on goal. All players are observed in both shooting and goalkeeping   techniques.

These three drills are just a few of the many exercises a coach can use to help identify good goalkeeping prospects, without compromising or depriving outfield players of quality time. I must stress at this point the importance of teaching all players the basics of catching, receiving low balls, and diving before exposing them to shot-stopping situations. Failure to do so may result in injury to the player placed in the goal.

After a few practice sessions, the coach should be able to identify two or three players as good potential goalkeepers. Even after goalkeepers have been chosen, they should get the opportunity to play other positions in order to gain a better understanding and appreciation of the game. I strongly suggest using goalkeepers in positions down the field (sweeper, center back, center half). These positions demand that the players read and direct the flow of the game from a perspective similar to that of a goalkeeper. Striker is also a very important position for the goalkeeper because here he observes how the goalkeeper's position can make scoring easier or more difficult.

In conclusion, the importance of the coach's decision to allow goalkeepers to experience playing in the field cannot be overstated, for several reasons:

1. Field play involves the goalkeeper in the rhythm and flow of the game, increasing his appreciation of the various factors that can be used to create goal-scoring opportunities.
2. It allows the goalkeeper variety and eases the pressure of always being the last player in the defense.
3. It allows the goalkeeper to master foot skills which are so important with the introduction of the back pass rule. The back pass rule states the goalkeeper cannot use his hands to field the ball when it is passed back to him by his teammates. His privileges of handling the ball ceases and he must now use any other part of the body except the hands.

Goalkeeping Technique

Technical proficiency is the cornerstone of a skillful goalkeeping performance. A large portion of the goalkeeper's work involves ball handling (i.e. catching, punching, deflecting, diving, throwing, and kicking). The quality goalkeeper is one who possesses the ability to perform these tasks efficiently and effectively while under pressure. The wider the goalkeeper's range or techniques and the greater his competence at each, the more confidently he is apt to perform. A confident goalkeeper instills confidence in his teammates and inspires them to play to the best of their ability.

Goalkeeping technique varies from person to person. Some factors which influence these variations include: physical characteristics, experience playing in the outfield positions, personality and nationality. For instance, some goalkeepers because of their national soccer heritage feel quite comfortable in catching a high ball (on a diving save) and immediately tucking the ball safely onto their body, then landing on the outside of the shoulder, hip and thigh. Others prefer to catch the ball and place it against the ground in order to break the fall. Goalkeepers in South America often elect to parry a chest high shot downward before regaining full control of the ball while some British goalkeepers believe firmly in catching the ball on the first touch.

Coaches should understand that goalkeepers — like their outfield teammates - vary in style from person to person and must be encouraged to develop their own natural style. If the goalkeeper consistently makes saves in a game utilizing an unorthodox technique, he should not be forced to change. The bottom line is to make the save. However, if goals are being scored as the result of technical errors made by the goalkeeper, then changes in technique are appropriate.

Although goalkeeping technique varies from person to person, and for the reasons explained earlier in the text, the following basic safety principles generally apply:

1. Focus the eyes on the ball until it is lodged safely in the hands.
2. Position the body behind the ball and in line with its flight.
3. Use both hands to catch the ball. They must be positioned behind the ball.
4. If in doubt about whether a ball is catchable, punch it to safety high, wide and with distance away from the goal.

The following section will explore the most widely accepted goalkeeping techniques.

Chapter 4

The Basic Starting Position

T he very nature of goalkeeping demands that the goalkeeper be prepared to move quickly in any direction — to dive, jump, stretch to reach high balls at a distance, move quickly to either side, or sprint explosively off the goal line. In order to perform these tasks effectively, the goalkeeper must assume a position allowing equal opportunity to field shots from different heights, angles and distances.

The Basic Ready Position

In Figure 4-1A, the goalkeeper's feet are positioned about shoulder width apart. The arms hang down at the sides, slightly away from the thighs, with the palms facing the thighs. The feet and knees face the oncoming ball.

In Figure 4-1B, the feet are aligned, with the body weight placed on the soles of the feet. The head is slightly ahead of the knees, so that the body is leaning forward ready to go after the ball. The arms hang down at the sides and slightly in front of the body with the palms facing the thighs. The legs are bent slightly at the knees. It is very important that the goalkeeper stand as tall as possible while keeping the knees slightly bent. Crouching too low will make the goalkeeper vulnerable to shots over his head. Standing upright without bending the knees reduces his ability to move quickly in any direction, especially to low shots.

Important Points To Note

- Keeping the hands at the sides gives the goalkeeper an equal opportunity to catch the ball effectively on low and high shots. Moving the hands slightly away from the body makes the target space (the goal) appear smaller, thus making the attacker's task more difficult. The goalkeeper should always "play big" — move off the goal line and stay on his feet as long as possible to reduce the target space. Refer to Chapter 11's discussion of angle play for other examples of playing big.
- To maintain good balance, the goalkeeper's body weight must be placed on the balls of the feet. The head must be held steady and positioned slightly in front of the shoulders and feet. In this position the goalkeeper should be relaxed and the legs should have enough tension in them so that they feel alive and ready for action.
- Despite the popular belief among goalkeepers that in order to be ready you must be on your toes, maximum explosive movements cannot be achieved from this position. For maximum explosive movements (diving, jumping, sprinting) always stand on the balls of the feet with the head slightly in front of the knees and feet at the

moment the ball is kicked. The often used coaching point "stay on your toes" really means to be alert, not literally stand on the toes.

Figure 4-1A

Figure 4-1B

Chapter 5

Fielding Low And Waist-high Shots

here are three basic methods of fielding ground shots: (1) the standing method (2) the kneeling method and, (3) the scoop-dive forward method. All other methods are merely variations of these three based on individual style and body structure.

The Standing Method

Figures 5-1A-D illustrate the standing method. In figure 5-1A the body is positioned behind the ball and the feet are slightly apart, but not enough for the ball to pass through. The legs are braced at the knees and the body is bent at the waist. The palms of both hands are positioned behind the ball, with the fingers under the ball. The wrists and forearms face the ball and are parallel to each other. The head is between the arms and directly over the ball. As soon as the ball makes contact with the hands (Fig. 5-1B), it is scooped up by cupping the hands under the ball. The wrists and forearms remain parallel and behind the ball. When the ball passes the base of the thumbs (Fig. 5-1C), it rolls up the "track" formed by the parallel forearms. The hands and fingers are behind the ball ready to pull it into the body. In figure 5-1D, the body is once again in the upright position with the ball tucked securely against the body. The hands and forearms are curled behind and around the ball to prevent it from slipping out.

Figure 5-1A   *Figure 5-1B*   *Figure 5-1C*   *Figure 5-1D*

The Kneeling Method

The kneeling method also requires that the body be positioned behind the ball. The goalkeeper places his right knee on the ground (sometimes the knee may be a few inches off the ground) behind and to the side of the ball (Fig. 5-2A). The front of the knee faces the heel of the opposite foot. The lower leg is perpendicular to the oncoming ball. The heel of the opposite (left) foot faces the grounded knee and the inside of the foot faces the oncoming ball. The distance between the grounded knee and the opposite leg should be small enough to keep the ball from slipping through should it escape through the hands.

The upper body is twisted to face the oncoming ball (Figs. 5-2A, 5-2B), and the arms are held parallel to each other in front of the body. The hands are positioned behind and under the ball. As the ball passes the base of the thumbs (Fig. 5-2B), it is scooped up and pulled against the body (Figs. 5-2C, 5-2D).

Figure 5-2A

Figure 5-2A Lateral

Figure 5-2B

Figure 5-2B Lateral

Figure 5-2C   *Figure 5-2D*

The Scoop and Dive Forward Method

The scoop and dive forward method is commonly used by modern goalkeepers. In figure 5-3A the goalkeeper lowers his body, with the hands behind and under the ball. As the ball makes contact with the hands, it is scooped up against the chest. Simultaneously, the rest of the body is dropped down against the ground and behind the ball thus forming a safety barrier protecting the ball from slipping through (Fig. 5-3B)

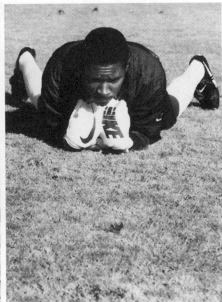

Figure 5-3Λ   *Figure 5-3B*   *Figure 5-3C*

Important Points About Low Shots

During games goalkeepers might not always be able to adhere strictly to textbook methods of fielding low shots. It is extremely important, however, to always position the hands behind and under the ball. The forearms must be paralleled to each other and behind the oncoming ball at all times, in order for the ball to be fielded cleanly and with one touch.

In order to reduce the incidence of balls dropping out or slipping through the hands, the goalkeeper should avoid "picking up" the ball (Fig. 5-4).

Goalkeepers in the kneeling position must avoid having the front of the knee facing the ball with the lower leg behind the body. The lower leg, when positioned sideways (as illustrated by Fig. 5-2B), forms an additional barrier behind the ball. Having the knee face the opposite foot reduces the chances of it accidentally hitting the ball, thus causing fumbles.

While these three methods are widely used, there are instances when one method is preferred over another. As a goalkeeper, I preferred the standing method for the following reasons:

1. It was comfortable for me. I was quite flexible and had no problems touching the ground with the palms of my hands.
2. On fielding the ball, I was able to spot open teammates and deliver quick counterattacking passes faster than when I used the other two methods.

On the other hand, the kneeling and the scoop and dive forward methods are preferred by some goalkeepers for the following reasons:

1. Their arms may be too short to touch the ground comfortably without bending the knees. This is often true of young goalkeepers (12-14 years) during their adolescent growth and of older goalkeepers with flexibility problems.
2. The goalkeeper prefers (for safety reasons) to lower his center of gravity in order to get the top half of the body closer to the ball and behind it.

Figure 5-4

Fielding Waist-high Shots

Shots arriving at waist height are probably the easiest to field. Following the basic principles of goalkeeping, the player in figure 5-5A positions his body behind the ball. His arms are extended to meet the oncoming ball. The palms of the hands face up. The forearms are parallel and approximately 3-6 inches apart (depending on the size of the forearms).

Before the catch is made, the hands are positioned below the ball with the palms facing up (Fig. 5-5B). When the ball passes the base of the thumbs the goalkeeper curls the hands from the wrists, quickly pulling the ball backward to the body (Fig. 5-5C). As the ball is received, the body sags in to absorb the impact and reduce the chance of the ball escaping. Note that the forearms and hands are positioned behind the ball, making it easier for the goalkeeper to gather the ball cleanly.

Important Points About Waist-high Shots

Positioning the hands under the ball and waiting until it passes the base of the thumbs before pulling it against the body are two important rules for gathering waist-high shots. Goalkeepers who apply them not only give themselves a more secure grip on the ball, but also reduce the chance of the fingers getting jammed during the catch.

Another safety practice which helps reduce the incidence of balls rebounding out of the hands is leaning the head forward and downward over the ball (Fig. 5-5C).

After the ball is collected, the forearms should remain under the ball and parallel to each other. Otherwise, the ball can slip through to the ground, giving opponents another chance to score.

When faced with powerful shots at a level above the ankles and below the knees, some goalkeepers choose to lower the body (by bending one knee a few inches from the ground) and gathering the ball in the same fashion as they would a waist-high shot.

A   B   C   *Lateral View of C*

Figure 5-5

31

Chapter 6

Catching And Jumping To Catch

I cannot emphasize how vital it is for the goalkeeper to catch the ball cleanly on the first touch, whether he is standing, jumping or diving full length. The need to control the ball from first contact is as critical in goal as it is up the field, since in both the goalkeeping and outfield positions, the better the ball control the more effective the player's performance. Because the nature of goalkeeping leaves little room for error, the goalkeeper must strive to eliminate untidiness by consistently catching the ball cleanly and with the first contact in all situations whether or not there is pressure.

Having established control by catching the ball, the goalkeeper must understand that he is in a very commanding position — no one can take the ball away and his team cannot go on the offensive until he puts the ball back into play. The goalkeeper must therefore endeavor to distribute the ball effectively. Chapter 9 discusses distribution but it is important to note that clean catching enhances distribution.

Principles of Catching

Always get behind and in line with the flight of the ball. In Figure 6-1A, the arms are extended forward and up toward the ball. The palms face the ball while the fingers are pointed up and slightly forward. Just as the ball is about to make contact with the hands, the forearms bend at the elbows. On contact (Fig. 6-1B), the hands form a barrier behind the ball. The forearms, bent at the elbows, are withdrawn quickly toward the face, cushioning the force of the shot. Note that the head is positioned behind the ball (Fig. 6-1C). Figure 6-1D illustrates the proper position of the hands at the

Figure 6-1A

Figure 6-1B

Figure 6-1C

Figure 6-1D

moment the ball is caught. The index fingers and thumbs of both hands combine to form a "W" behind the ball. The midline of the ball should make contact with the base of the fingers while the "strong thumbs" positioned behind the ball act as a safety valve to prevent balls from slipping through. There should be no space between the hands and the ball.

Important Points to Note

(a) In catching the ball, the goalkeeper must position his body behind and in line with the flight of the ball. Reception occurs in front of the face (Fig. 6-1B). The head is positioned behind the ball and between the arms, as if looking through a window (Fig. 6-1C).

(b) Receiving the ball in front of the face enables the goalkeeper to offset the impact of the shot by withdrawing the forearms and hands toward the face.

(c) Getting in line with the flight of the ball enables the goalkeeper to have full view of the ball all the way into the hands.

(d) On contact, the arms and hands must be relaxed. If they are stiff, they will create a firm surface from which the ball can rebound. The arms and hands should not, however, be too relaxed because that might allow a hard shot to slip through the hands.

(e) Work on being a two-handed goalkeeper — try to get two hands behind the ball whenever possible. Catch the ball cleanly and with one touch. After catching the ball, hold on to it firmly. Strive at all times to eliminate second touches, fumbles, and downward deflections because loose balls offer attackers extra chances to score.

Jumping to Catch a High Ball

Determining when to come off the goal line to intercept a high ball is a skill vital to effective goalkeeping. Jumping to catch a high ball is a very important technique which the goalkeeper must develop and master in order to successfully deal with high crosses. Intercepting a high ball combines two techniques: jumping and catching.

The objective is to catch the ball at the highest point of the goalkeeper's jump. For instructional purposes the technique of jumping to catch a high ball is divided into three phases: (a) the preparatory phase; (b) the execution; and (c) the landing

The Preparatory Phase

As illustrated in Figure 6-2A, the goalkeeper should move off the goal line with an explosive extension of the rear leg. The right arm is driven forward as the opposite arm is pulled back. In order to drive the body forward effectively, the top half of the body must be leaning forward with the head trying to catch up with the knee of the forward leg. The explosive extension of the rear leg provides the needed push to propel the body toward the ball. As the goalkeeper gets closer to the ball, the body moves to a slightly more upright position (Fig. 6-2B). Just before takeoff (Fig. 6-2C), the player makes a long last stride. This long step (similar to that of a high jumper prior to takeoff) decreases the body's forward momentum and lowers the center of gravity. The top half of the body is positioned slightly behind the flexed knee of the forward leg. The arms swing down and back, further decreasing the forward momentum, and the head moves to a position slightly behind the flexed knee of the forward leg.

At takeoff (Fig. 6-2D) the body is propelled off the ground by an explosive extension of the grounded leg and an upward driving action of the opposite knee. The extension of the grounded leg provides the "push" to launch the body upward while the opposite leg provides the "pull" lifting the body up toward the ball. Simultaneously, the arms drive forward and upward, providing an additional lifting action that helps the goalkeeper achieve greater height and the hands move to an open position to receive the ball as it falls. The opening of the hands is accompanied by a full extension of the arms. The palms are positioned behind and under the ball. The head is held between the arms with the eyes focused intently on the ball (Fig. 6-2E).

A   B   C   D

E   F   G

Figure 6-2

35

The Execution

The catch is made at the apex of the goalkeeper's jump. The hands are positioned behind and under the ball.(Fig. 6-2E). The head is between the arms and slightly behind the ball. Holding the knee in front of the body protects the goalkeeper from onrushing attackers. After the ball is caught, it is brought in and held safely against the body.

Landing

After catching the ball (Fig. 6-2F), the goalkeeper is now ready to land. The takeoff leg touches the ground first, followed closely by the opposite leg. Upon contact with the ground, both legs are bent to cushion the impact of landing (Fig. 6-2G). The ball is still securely against the body. In a crowded area, however, the goalkeeper should be careful not to pull the ball down too quickly lest it be dislodged by another player who is contesting for the ball. Instead, he should hold the ball as high as possible until it can be brought down safely without making contact with anyone (Fig. 6-3).

Figure 6-3

Important Points To Note

(a) The long last stride (Fig. 6-2C) before takeoff is vital in attaining maximum height because it reduces forward momentum and, at the same time, lowers the body's center of gravity.

(b) The forward and upward swinging of the arms helps the goalkeeper gain height providing "pull."

(c) The forward and upward swinging of the leg opposite the takeoff leg also helps the goalkeeper attain maximum height after takeoff (Fig. 6-2D).

(d) The knee held in front of the body serves as a fender, protecting the goalkeeper against oncoming attackers. However, the goalkeeper should avoid raising his knees in the following situations: (1) when he has a teammate directly in front of him (the knee-up technique may damage a teammate) and, (2) when teammates and opponents closely surround the goalkeeper, the raised knee may get caught under someone's arm, thus impeding the goalkeeper's ability to reach the high ball effectively.

In situations such as these two mentioned above, the traditional knee-up technique must give way to a more practical way of getting to the ball: An unorthodox jump from off both feet, similar to jumping for a basketball rebound, may prove to be the most effective method of getting to the ball and also sparing a teammate a knee in the back.

Chapter 7

Diving

A diving save is one of the most spectacular moments in a soccer game, equaled only by the excitement of a goal being scored. However, diving is one of the most complicated goalkeeping techniques to teach and master. There are several reasons why this is so:

- There are many different diving reactions to the variety of shots taken on goal.
- The natural fear of hitting the ground and of the pain that follows contact makes many goalkeepers land incorrectly.
- Most coaches are not familiar with the mechanics of diving and so are unable to teach proper technique.

It is therefore unwise to set hard and fast rules when teaching goalkeepers the proper mechanics of diving. Indeed, one principle can be right in one instance and totally inappropriate or impossible to execute in another.

Goalkeepers who consistently hurt themselves diving end up being "ground shy," afraid of making contact with the ground when diving to save low or high shots. As a result they sometimes elect to use their feet to stop shots or avoid diving altogether. Of course many quality goalkeepers have made great saves with their feet, but beginning goalkeepers must be trained to dive and use both hands as often as possible. Use of the feet to make a save is an instinctive reaction and should be used in emergency situations only and never as a substitute for diving. The goalkeeper who is competent in the art of diving minimizes goal scoring possibilities by being able to cover more of the goal.

Because diving is so important to effective goalkeeping and because many coaches are not familiar with proper diving mechanics, this chapter covers several different methods. Each is discussed relative to the type of shot it can stop most effectively. For further clarification I have categorized the various situations in which a diving save is necessary.

It is important that coaches expose young goalkeepers to all the methods of diving described in this chapter, and allow them to select the one that yields the most success. A variety of factors — from the goalkeeper's body type and physical fitness level to ground conditions — all play important roles in determining which method is most suitable.

Shots Near the Body

Ground shots traveling 12-24 inches to the side of the goalkeeper's feet appear to be relatively easy to save, but in fact, they are among the most difficult. If the goalkeeper, in an attempt to get the top half of his body down behind the ball, gets down too late, the ball can roll under the body and into the goal. The biggest task here is to get the body down to the ground behind the ball in the quickest time.

In Figure 7-1, the goalkeeper collapses the leg closest to the ball, falling downward behind the ball (Fig. 7-2).

There are times when a point-blank shot cannot be stopped by diving. In this case, the goalkeeper may elect to use his feet. However, it is recommended that the hands and body be used in diving whenever possible.

Aerial shots can be divided into categories: those around waist height, and those shoulder high and above.

Waist-high shots can be stopped using a relatively simple technique. But the goalkeeper must always remember how vital it is to dive sideways, keeping the head steady and positioned behind the arms at all times. In Figure 7-3A the shot is coming in to the goalkeeper's right side. He makes a quick step laterally with the foot closest to the ball. In Figure 7-3B, the goalkeeper makes the catch as his body weight shifts laterally, thus transferring his body weight over to the foot nearest the ball. In Figure 7-3C the goalkeeper is on his way downward in preparation for landing. Many goalkeepers use this method of landing, but others prefer to pull the ball onto the body after the catch, then land on the outside of the upper leg, hip, body and shoulder (Fig. 7-3E).

The principles for saving a head-high shot are basically the same as for saving a waist-high shot. In Figure 7-4A, the goalkeeper moves sideways. When the top of the body has traveled well past the grounded leg, the body is now in the optimum position for takeoff (Fig. 7-4B). The catch is made with the goalkeeper's body facing front, head between the arms and hands behind the ball (Fig. 7-4C). Note that the front of the body faces the ball. On landing, the goalkeeper may elect to use either of the two landing methods illustrated in Figures 7-3D and 7-3E.

Figure 7-1

Figure 7-2

Figure 7-3A

Figure 7-3B

Figure 7-3C

Figure 7-3D

Figure 7-3E

Figure 7-4A

Figure 7-4B

Figure 7-4C

Shots Well Away From The Body

There is no more breathtaking sight than that of a goalkeeper flying through the air, body parallel to the ground, cleanly catching a well-placed shot intended for the uppermost corner of the goal. However, high diving to save shots well away from the body demands a great deal of explosive leg strength, courage and a competitive attitude. Whenever I was preparing to save a shot, I would say to myself, "Wherever you put it, I am going to get it." The goalkeeper must be completely unafraid of making contact with the ground. Anticipation, mobility, coordination, timing and sound diving mechanics are all of supreme importance to effective diving.

There are four critical stages of diving to save a shot well away from the body:

• The takeoff
• Flight
• The catch
• Landing

The proper execution of these stages varies with the type of incoming shot.

Ground Shots

The Takeoff — In order to execute an efficient dive, the goalkeeper must first assume the proper starting position: feet comfortably apart, weight balanced evenly on soles of the feet, knees slightly flexed, arms at the sides with the palms facing the thighs, head steady, and eyes focused on the ball (Fig. 7-5A).

Immediately after the shot is taken, the goalkeeper must move the foot nearest the ball laterally (Fig. 7-5B). The feet and knees face the front and the arms remain at the sides. In Figure 7-5C, the body weight is transferred over the foot closest to the ball. The far leg extends, pushing the body toward the ball (note that the feet, knees, and body still face the front). As the top half of the body travels well past the ballside foot (Fig. 7-5D), the body is now in optimum takeoff position. The leg farthest from the ball is fully extended and the head and shoulders point toward the ball's flight path. The leg closest to the ball is now fully flexed. An explosive extension of the left leg launches the body in a straight line toward the ball.

The Catch and Landing — Figure 7-5E illustrates the catch and the landing. The goalkeeper's body is still facing outward. Both hands are behind the ball, forming a defensive wall. When the ball reaches the hands, the catch is made utilizing the same basic catching principles for a high shot as illustrated in Chapter 6. For example, the hands form a basket behind the ball; the midpoint of the ball makes contact with a point just below the base of the fingers, the thumbs are positioned behind the ball, and the fingers are wrapped securely around the ball to ensure its safety. To further ensure that the ball is caught cleanly, the goalkeeper can use the top hand to squeeze the ball against the ground.

After the ball is caught, the goalkeeper draws it toward the body, and at the same time pulls the knees toward the chest, protecting the ball from oncoming attackers.

Upon landing, the outer aspect of the thigh hits the ground first, followed by the hip, rib cage, and finally the shoulders. This landing sequence serves a dual purpose: it presents a large surface area to absorb the fall, reducing the chance of injury, and it

Figure 7-5A

Figure 7-5B

Figure 7-5C

Figure 7-5D

Figure 7-5E

leaves the hands free to gather the ball. Note that the body is positioned on the ground behind the ball. The goalkeeper is also lying on his side, head between the arms, eyes focused on the ball and the palms facing the oncoming ball.

Aerial Shots

There are two types of aerial shots: short range shots that allow no time for preliminary steps before takeoff (i.e. the goalkeeper has to propel his body sideways and upward from the basic starting position); and those that allow preliminary steps (i.e. shots from well outside the penalty area). The diving response which the goalkeeper selects depends on the amount of time he has to prepare for the shot.

Power Dive

To execute this graceful and breathtaking technique, the goalkeeper's main objective should be to generate sufficient power to enable him to achieve the necessary height, speed and distance to catch the ball cleanly with both hands. If he is unable to catch the ball with both hands he should elect to use one hand to deflect the ball around the upright or over the crossbar. In either case every part of the body must be utilized properly. Timing, explosive power, coordination and position of the hands are key factors.

Figures 7-6A through 7-6G help the reader better understand the important components of the high diving technique: preparation (Figs. 7-6A, 7-6B), takeoff (Fig. 7-6C), execution (Figs. 7-6D), and landing (Figs. 7-6E, 7-6F).

Preparation — The goalkeeper is in the starting position, his body well balanced on the balls of the feet, ready to go after the ball in any direction. The goalkeeper must develop the ability to determine as soon as possible the flight of the ball and the direction in which it is traveling. The sooner he can begin tracking the shot, the better his chances are of intercepting it. In Figure 7-6A the body weight has shifted over the leg closest to the ball. The center of gravity has been lowered by the flexing of the knees, placing the body in a crouched position. Simultaneously with the flexing of the knees, the arms should swing rhythmically downward. In Figure 7-6B the body weight is well over the flexed ballside leg. The goalkeeper is now ready for takeoff.

Takeoff — The takeoff phase begins when the goalkeeper explosively extends the leg closest to the ball (Fig. 7-6C). This explosive extension provides distance. As the ballside

A   B   C

Figure 7-6

leg is extended, the opposite bent leg is pulled upward and driven powerfully in the direction of the ball. This upward movement of the far leg helps the goalkeeper achieve height by lifting the center of gravity off the ground and allowing parallel extension of the torso. The driving motion of the knee toward the ball (as if the player is attempting to kick the ball with his knee) also helps increase the distance of the dive.

The arms also play a significant role in takeoff, specifically in achieving height and distance. As the takeoff leg extends, the arms swing up toward the ball.

Coordination of these movements — leaning toward the ball before takeoff, explosive extension of takeoff leg, lifting the opposite leg, and the accompanying arm movements — is of the utmost importance in the takeoff phase of the power dive.

Execution — Figure 7-6D shows the goalkeeper traveling through the air toward the ball. Note that the body is sideways with the front facing the oncoming ball. In this position the player has an unobstructed view of the oncoming ball.

In Figure 7-6D the goalkeeper makes the catch. Notice the hands positioned behind the ball, as they were in the illustration of catching a head-high shot. The head is positioned between the arms and the ball is in full view as it makes contact with the hands.

Now, the job is half done. The goalkeeper has successfully taken off and made a clean two-handed catch. The other half of the task is landing safely while holding on to the ball securely (not allowing it to bounce out of his hands on landing).

Landing — Figures 7-6E and 7-6F illustrate methods of landing. A goalkeeper who has the time to pull the ball in to his body might elect to use the method illustrated by Figure 7-6E. Having caught the ball he immediately pulls it in to the body to secure it from bouncing out on landing.

The goalkeeper lands on the side of the thigh, hip, rib cage and arm/shoulder. Players who land this way are less likely to be injured since the fall is absorbed by a large surface area.

On harder surfaces, it might be advisable to use the landing method illustrated by Figure 7-6F. First contact with the ground is made with the ball, which is wedged between the hands and the ground. This method significantly cushions the impact of landing.

D   *E*   *F*

These two techniques of landing are used frequently by goalkeepers throughout the world. Young goalkeepers should be exposed to both methods and allowed to choose the one they are most comfortable with.

Power Dive with Crossover Step(s)

Sometimes the goalkeeper has enough time to take a preliminary step or two toward the ball before diving to save a high shot. These few steps enable the goalkeeper to gain more momentum and therefore more height and distance on his dive than the power dive from a standing position.

Figure 7-7 illustrates the power dive with crossover step(s). In Figure 7-7A the goalkeeper makes a quick step toward the ball with his left foot. This initial movement is followed closely by a crossover step (Fig. 7-7B) as the right leg is brought across the front of the left leg. In the final step before takeoff (Fig. 7-7C), the left leg is moved laterally behind the right leg, bringing the goalkeeper to an effective ready position — feet parallel to each other and just a little more than shoulder width apart, and the front of the body facing outward. As the body weight passes well over the left takeoff foot, the body is propelled toward the ball with an explosive extension of the takeoff leg (Fig. 7-7D). The momentum created by the preliminary steps coupled with the swinging-upward movement of the arms and right leg, enables the goalkeeper to get maximum height and distance on his dive.

During a game the goalkeeper, based on the position of his feet and body weight, may elect to use the first step with either the foot closest to the ball (Fig. 7-7A) or the foot farthest from the ball (Fig. 7-7B).

The diving save is the stock in the goalkeeper's trade. Preparation, quick feet, explosive leg power and sound diving mechanics are essential requirements for effective diving.

Important Points About Ground Shots Near the Body

Always try to dive sideways, with the front of the body facing the ball. By using a sideways dive:

a. The goalkeeper can go to ground faster.
b. The palms of the hands and the front of the body face the ball, presenting a larger barrier behind the ball.
c. Adequate vision is assured.
d. The side of the body cushions the fall, leaving the hands free to save the ball.
e. It is easy to adhere to the principles of catching: hands on the ball, index fingers and thumbs forming a "W" and the head positioned between the arms.

A goalkeeper who dives and lands on his stomach should anticipate the following problems:

a. The ball traveling across his line of vision — hindering adequate vision.
b. The hands facing downward just prior to the catch leaving no safety barrier behind the ball.
c. Injury caused by landing on the stomach, such as diving on top of the ball, hitting the ground with the stomach, or using the elbow or hand to break the fall.

Figure 7-7A

Figure 7-7B

Figure 7-7C

Figure 7-7D

When collecting aerial shots the goalkeeper must:

a. Dive sideways to get the body behind the flight of the ball.
b. Try to get two hands on the ball whenever possible.
c. Take the shortest route to the ball — a straight line.
d. Either land on as broad a surface as possible — the outside of a leg, hip, body, arm, shoulder — or use the ball as a wedge against the ground to absorb the impact of the fall.

Important Points About Shots Away From The Body

Power Dive From The Standing Position

The goalkeeper must use every part of the body to help attain maximum speed, height and distance.

a. The position of the body before takeoff is critical. The body weight should be transferred to the leg closest to the ball until the body is at an angle of 40-60 degrees (depending on the height of the shot).
b. The body should be launched by an explosive extension of the takeoff leg. The arms should swing upward (toward the ball) along with the knee of the leg farthest from the ball.

Power Dive From A Moving Position.

The two-step crossover — The goalkeeper passes the leg farthest from the ball in front of the grounded leg. As the weight is transferred to the front leg, the rear leg is moved in the direction of the ball, and the takeoff is made.

The three-step crossover — Essentially the same as the two-step crossover, but an extra step is made with the foot closest to the ball.

Chapter 8

Deflecting And Punching

Sometimes the goalkeeper has no alternative but to deflect, punch, or parry the ball to safety. This chapter deals with the mechanics of deflecting and punching.

Deflecting Around the Uprights

Ground Shots

Sometimes ground shots are too wide for the goalkeeper to catch. Instead, he might be able to get one hand to the ball, or even just the fingertips. In such situations, the goalkeeper should reach with the arm closest to the ball (Fig. 8-1A). The goalkeeper can achieve more distance on his dive using the hand that is closer to the ball. The palm of the hand should face the front and be positioned behind the ball. On contact the ball is pushed safely to the side of the uprights with the heel of the hand (Fig. 8-1B). Sometimes the shot is a bit too far away for the goalkeeper to get the heel of the hand behind the ball. In this case the fingers are relied upon to make the deflection (Fig. 8-1C). In this situation, the wrist and fingers are locked. Just before contact is made the fingers are pulled forward, deflecting the ball around the upright. The important muscles involved in deflecting shots are the muscles around the wrist, hand and the fingers. The goalkeeper should not neglect the development of these muscles for with strong wrist, hand and finger muscles even the slightest touch will alter the direction of a shot enough to deprive an attacker of a goal.

Figure 8-1A

Figure 8-1B

Figure 8-1C

Aerial Shot

The first objective in dealing with high shots and crosses is to catch the ball cleanly, thus preventing a corner kick. However, there are instances when the goalkeeper is compelled to deflect the ball over the crossbar or around the uprights. Four categories of shots come to mind:

1. Powerfully driven shots above waist height and to the side of the goalkeeper
2. Powerfully driven shots above head height
3. High crosses near the goal
4. Incoming balls dropping behind the goalkeeper

Whenever possible, the goalkeeper should use both hands to deflect powerful shots over the crossbar. More experienced goalkeepers, however, are able to use one hand quite effectively. The one-handed technique is sometimes preferred because it allows the goalkeeper to gain more height than with the two hands. In both methods the palms of the hands should be used to deflect the ball. It is very risky to attempt to punch the ball over the bar with the front of the knuckles — the contact area is smaller than that of the open palm and the risk of injury to the knuckle is high.

Shots Above the Waist — Figure 8-2 illustrates the technique involved in deflecting an above-waist-height shot around the upright. In Figure 8-2A the goalkeeper makes a lateral step with the foot closest to the ball (left foot). When his body weight travels well past the grounded leg (Fig. 8-2B) the body is propelled toward the oncoming ball. While traveling through the air (Fig. 8-2C) the body faces the front, the arm closest to the ball is fully extended and the palm of the hand is facing the ball. On contact the ball is deflected around the upright.

Figure 8-2A   Figure 8-2B   Figure 8-2C

Shots Above the Head — Whenever possible, the goalkeeper should use both hands to deflect head-high shots over the crossbar. More experienced goalkeepers, however are able to use one hand quite effectively. The one-handed technique is sometimes preferred because it allows the goalkeeper to gain more height than with two hands.

Powerful Shots — Figure 8-3A illustrates the technique of deflecting the ball over the crossbar with both hands. The wrists are locked with the fingers pointing upward and slightly backwards in the direction the ball is expected to travel. On contact the hands are positioned behind and slightly under the ball (Fig. 8-3B). The ball is then deflected over the bar. If the shot is struck powerfully and upward and these rules (locked wrists, hands under and behind the ball, and fingers pointed backwards and upward) are followed, the ball will be deflected safely over the crossbar.

Figure 8-3A   Figure 8-3B

Figure 8-4A shows the one-handed technique of deflecting the ball over the crossbar. The rules are identical to that of the two-handed method. The only difference is that one hand is used instead of two. Sometimes shots on goal may be too high for the goalkeeper to position the palm of his hand behind and under the ball as illustrated in Figure 8-1B. The fingers of the hand may be utilized to deflect the ball over the crossbar similar to the deflection method illustrated in Figure 8-1C. Figure 8-4B illustrates "tipping" the ball over the crossbar. Just before the ball makes contact with the fingers, the hand is positioned behind and under the ball with the fingers pointing upward and slightly backward. Upon contact the wrist must be locked along with the joints on each finger. The forward movement of the hand and the locking of the joints of the wrist and fingers provide enough resistance behind and under the ball to cause the shot to be deflected upward and over the crossbar (Fig. 8-4C).

Figure 8-4A   Figure 8-4B   Figure 8-4C

High Crosses Near the Goal — The goalkeeper in Figure 8-5 contacts the ball at the highest point of his jump. He can use either the hand closest to the field (Fig. 8-5A) or the one closest to the goal (Fig. 8-5B).

Figure 8-5A

Figure 8-5B

Balls Dropping Behind the Goalkeeper — Some shots are lofted over the goalkeeper's head, dropping down dangerously toward the goal. When this situation occurs the goalkeeper must utilize quick footwork to recover goalwards. In Figure 8-6A, the goalkeeper makes a drop step (step backward) with the left foot. The right shoulder faces the oncoming ball. The hand closest to the field is positioned under the ball lifting it over the crossbar (Fig 8-6B).

Note in Figure 8-6C the whole body is turned toward the goal as the goalkeeper follows the ball all the way over the crossbar. Inexperienced goalkeepers find it very difficult to deal with balls dropping behind them. Their big problem here is that they try to run backward with their backs facing the goal and are unable to gain maximum height and to follow the flight of the ball as it passes over their heads.

It is very important to understand that the technique of throwing the ball over the crossbar as illustrated in Figures 8-6A and 8-6B is only appropriate when the goalkeeper is

Figure 8-6A   *Figure 8-6B*   *Figure 8-6C*   *Figure 8-6D*

positioned between the ball and the goal or when the ball is directly over the head. If the ball, for whatever reason, is positioned nearer to the goal line than the goalkeeper and dipping dangerously under the crossbar, then the hand closest to the goal (the left hand) should be used to deflect the ball over the crossbar (Fig. 8-6D). If the hand closest to the field (right hand) is used in an attempt to make the save the chances are that the ball would be pulled down into the goal. The reasons for using the left hand are as follows:

a. the left hand can get to the ball quicker than the right.
b. the left hand is the only hand that can be positioned between the goal and the ball.
c. the left hand is under the ball and in a good position to deflect the ball over the crossbar

Punching

If the goalkeeper is unsure of catching a high lofted center because (a) players are blocking his path to the ball, (b) he is unable to reach the ball with both hands, or (c) of slippery conditions, he should elect to punch the ball to safety away from the goal, high and wide. One or two hands can be used to punch the ball.

Two-Hand Punch

This method is generally recommended for young players because of the size of the knuckles and high risk of injury when one fist is used — the larger the surface area the less the risk of injury or mistakes. Many experienced goalkeepers, however, prefer the two-handed method when they are able to reach the ball with both hands, especially those high centers traveling toward the goal. Figure 8-7 illustrates the two-hand technique. Both fists are tightly clenched, forming a flat, broad surface, while the inner aspects of the wrists face each other. The forearms are bent at the elbows (Fig. 8-7A). When the ball gets into striking distance, the goalkeeper extends the arms making contact with the ball with the front of both knuckles (Fig. 8-7B) and punches through the ball until the arms are fully extended (Fig. 8-7C).

Figure 8-7A   *Figure 8-7B*   *Figure 8-7C*

Figure 8-8A

Figure 8-8B

Figure 8-8C

Figure 8-8D

One-Hand Punch

Sometimes it is not possible for the goalkeeper to reach a high center with two hands, i.e. in a crowded area or when the ball is too far away from the body. When such situations occur the goalkeeper may elect to punch the ball with one hand. The one-hand punch is also used effectively when punching crossballs (Fig. 8-8). At all times the knuckles must be held firmly, with a flat surface and the wrist locked firmly.

In Figure 8-8A a ball is lofted from the left side of the field. The task of the goalkeeper is to punch the ball to the opposite side of the field. The goalkeeper times the cross and takes off on one foot. The right arm is bent at the elbow in preparation to make contact with the ball.

As the ball gets into punching distance (Fig. 8-8B), the goalkeeper extends his forearm and punches the ball to the opposite side of the field.

In Figure 8-8C, the goalkeeper follows through with the hand pointing in the direction of the punch.

Sometimes, however, in a crowded goal area, crosses may be driven in and curve dangerously to the near post. The only recourse the goalkeeper might have is to use the hand closest to the ball and punch it back in the same direction from which it came. (Fig. 8-8D).

Chapter 9

Distribution

When a goalkeeper is in possession of the ball, he is in an excellent position to initiate an attack by distributing the ball (throwing or kicking) accurately to teammates or in an area where they have an advantage over their opponents. Indeed, a good accurate pass from the goalkeeper represents the first line of attack. In order to distribute the ball effectively he must be competent in all phases of distribution. This chapter deals with the two methods of distribution - throwing and kicking.

Throwing

Overarm Throw

Throwing is the most accurate method of distribution. For long distances the overarm throw is most effective (Figs. 9-1A to 9-2D). In Figure 9-1A, the goalkeeper clutches the ball against the forearm to keep it secure. The palm of the hand is held below the ball and the player is about to step forward with the opposite foot. The left shoulder and arm both point to the direction of the intended pass. Just as the left foot touches the ground the right arm begins its upward movement (Fig. 9-1B). The ball is brought

Figure 9-1A   *Figure 9-1B*   *Figure 9-1C*   *Figure 9-1D*

Figure 9-2A   *Figure 9-2B*   *Figure 9-2C*

upward in a circular motion, the throwing arm is held straight and the ball is about to be released (Fig. 9-1C). Note that the throwing arm is still straight and the ball is above head height. After releasing the ball, the player's throwing arm points in the direction of the intended target (Fig. 9-1D). I have seen goalkeepers attempt long throws using a sidearm method. This method is not as accurate as the overarm method because the player has the tendency to swing the throwing arm across the body thus causing the ball to swerve sometimes away from the intended target.

For shorter distances the javelin throw is most effective. In Figure 9-2A, the player steps forward with the left foot and simultaneously draws the ball backward, slightly above head height, with the right hand. The hand is positioned behind the ball and the arm is bent at the elbow. In Figure 9-2B the ball is brought forward with a short sharp thrust and released just as it passes the head. In the followthrough (Fig. 9-2C), the throwing arm follows the direction of the pass.

Underarm Throw

The underarm throw is also useful in passing to teammates at short distances, usually in quick counterattack throws to the outside fullbacks. The player in Figure 9-3A is about to initiate an underarm throw. With the ball held securely against the wrist of his right hand he is about to step forward with the right foot. As he steps forward with the left foot (Fig. 9-3B), the ball is withdrawn backward and upward. As the left foot makes contact with the ground (Fig. 9-3C) the player swings the ball downward in a circular motion. The ball is about to be released. Note how the player has lowered his center of gravity in an effort to release the ball as low to the ground as possible (bowling action) (Fig. 9-3C). In the followthrough both knees are bent as the throwing arm follows the path of the ball (Fig. 9-3D).

The quality of the throw, when using the over- and underarm methods, should be uppermost in the goalkeeper's mind. Even the most accurate throw is worthless if it is thrown too hard for a teammate to control, or if there is very little for him to do once he is in possession of the ball. In other words the ball should always be delivered in such a manner that teammates are able to do something with it.

Kicking

The goalkeeper can distribute the ball over longer distances by kicking because the leg muscles are bigger and stronger than those of the arm. There are two types of kicks

Figure 9-3A

Figure 9-3B

Figure 9-3C

Figure 9-3D

which a goalkeeper can utilize in making long passes (over 50 yards): (1) volley and (2) half-volley. In the volley kick the ball is kicked before it touches the ground. For the half-volley, the ball makes contact with the ground before it is kicked. The goalkeeper, however, has to decide which kick is more effective during the game and must attempt to kick the ball where his teammates have a good chance of receiving the ball.

Figure 9-4A

Figure 9-4B

Figure 9-4C

Figure 9-4D

Figure 9-4E

Figure 9-4F

Volley Kick

For instructional purposes the kicking method is broken down into five parts: (a) the release; (b) a step forward with the non-kicking leg; (c) the forward swing of the kicking leg; (d) the contact; and (e) the followthrough.

The Release — To gain maximum distance on the kick two types of release are commonly used by goalkeepers: the two-hand release and the one-hand (hand opposite to the kicking leg) release. For the two-hand release (Fig. 9-4A) the player holds the ball with two hands, throws it forward and upward and at the same time takes a step forward with the right foot. For the one-hand release (Fig. 9-4B), the player holds the ball with the left hand and throws it forward and upward and at the same time steps forward with the right foot.

Step Forward — The player in Figure 9-4C makes the second step forward with the left foot and pulls the right leg backward from the hip.

Forward Swing — The right leg is pulled forward and the lower leg is about to be extended through the ball (Fig. 9-4D).

The Contact — On contact (Fig. 9-4E) the instep is driven through the bottom half of the ball, propelling it upward.

Followthrough — After kicking the ball, the force generated by the explosive extension of the lower leg causes the non-kicking leg to be pulled off the ground while the left arm swings forward and across the body as a counterbalance to the kicking leg (Fig. 9-4F). The position of the instep indicates the path of the ball — upward and forward.

Half-Volley

Figures 9-5A to 9-5D offer a lateral perspective of the half-volley in order to provide a good view of the proper technique involved when the kicking foot makes contact with the ball. The player in Figure 9-5A releases the ball (two-handed or one-handed) while stepping forward. The left leg comes forward and lands on the heel (Fig. 9-5B) as the right leg is pulled back at the hip.

In Figure 9-5C contact is made a fraction of a second after the ball touches the ground. Note the position of the instep (facing the ball) and the ankle (locked firmly). The kicking leg is swung through the bottom half of the ball as the body leans backward. Contact is made with the instep pointing forward and upward (Fig. 9-5D).

Possession is one of the most important facets of the attack. Therefore, when kicking, the goalkeeper must consider where the ball is going and to whom. In every case the objective should be to provide teammates with the greatest possible chance of retaining possession of the ball.

As the goalkeeper's kicking range improves, he must be careful to not out-kick his own strikers. Power is important, but accurate placement is essential to an effective attack.

Figure 9-5A

Figure 9-5B

Figure 9-5C

Figure 9-5D

Goalkeeping Tactics

If a goalkeeper expects to play a significant role in directing the course of the game, he must understand the function of his defenders and be capable of reading the opposition's attacking movements as they develop. A quality goalkeeper is able to analyze dangerous situations and plug up gaps in the defense by communicating effectively with his teammates. He must also be adept at coming off the goal line to intercept dangerous through passes and crosses.

Looking back over my own goalkeeping career, I can vividly recall the coaches and soccer enthusiasts who played a significant role in helping me become more aware of the importance of reading the game. In my late teens, I was blessed with sharp reflexes, good hands and above average agility and flexibility. There was hardly a shot that I was unable to save, yet in some games I played brilliantly while in others I was only mediocre. I knew something was missing, but I could not put my finger on it. While I thought it was a mental problem such as overconfidence or relaxing too much following an outstanding performance, it was something else. It took me more than two years to discover my deficiency — the inability to read and direct the game.

The first person to enlighten me was Kelvin "Pa" Aleong, an elderly scholar of the game in my country, Trinidad and Tobago. He had never been a coach, but could pinpoint flaws in a player's performance in any sport. Pa Aleong explained to me that I was concerned only with the shot blocking aspect of goalkeeping. He advised me to focus more attention on reading the game by observing dangerous situations (unmarked players, gaps in the defense); increasing my ability to communicate these observations to my teammates; and anticipating through passes and crossballs and cutting them off.

Being a quick learner, I soon put these tactical skills to good use. But there was still something missing in my game. The final piece of the puzzle fell into place after I consulted with two of the finest goalkeepers in Trinidad and Tobago, Joseph "Joey" Gonzalves and Cax Baptiste. Joey was short (5'7") and always seemed to be composed even in the most stressful situations. He made diving virtually unnecessary because of his excellent positioning. Cax on the other hand, weighed over 200 pounds, and was bowlegged. Although he seemed a bit overweight and slow, Cax was able to get his hands to almost any shot on goal, and, like Joey, he rarely dove to stop shots on goal.

After consulting and observing these two fine goalkeepers, I realized that they combined good positioning and keen anticipation to create the illusion of ease. I incorporated these two tactical principles into my game and was amazed at the improvement in the consistency of my play. I must add at this point that it took me more than a year and a half of dedicated hard work before I was able to develop good positioning and keen anticipation.

This section of the book discusses the tactical aspect of the game and reflects my trial and error experiences over years of playing against some of the best players in the world.

Chapter 10

Laws That Goalkeepers Should Know

A goalkeeper who is to play a vital role in directing the game must be fully aware of soccer laws, especially those affecting him the most. I have observed many situations in which goalkeepers allowed goals from free kicks by (a) mistaking a direct free kick infringement for an indirect kick, or (b) misreading how to respond to the back pass rule. This chapter deals with the laws that affect the goalkeeper most profoundly.

Equipment

FIFA Law IV (3) states that "the goalkeeper shall wear colors which distinguish him from the other players and from the referee." The reason for this law is that the goalkeeper is the only player on the field allowed to use his hands (in the penalty area only). If the goalkeeper's jersey is the same or similar to that of the other players, the referee could easily mistake the goalkeeper in a crowded penalty area for a defender and award a penalty kick for a handball violation when he handles the ball.

Coaches should familiarize themselves with the opposing team's colors before match day, or at least one hour before kickoff. On match days goalkeepers should always travel with two jerseys of different colors, just in case the referee calls for a change. There is nothing more unnerving than wearing someone else's jersey, especially if it is the wrong size or a color you dislike. I was playing with my national team (Trinidad and Tobago) in a World Cup qualifying game against Suriname. Our administrators were unaware of a recent rule change by FIFA forbidding goalkeepers from wearing all-black uniforms, which were reserved for referees. The game was delayed for more than 15 minutes while our manager searched for an alternate color jersey. This situation was very unnerving to me. First, the start of the game was delayed; second, the replacement shirt given to me was light blue (definitely my least favorite color) and a size too small.

The late start of the game — coupled with the shock of not being able to wear my lucky, favorite black jersey — threw my concentration off completely. Needless to say, the first half of the game was a complete disaster for me. I nervously dropped easy shots on goal and hesitated on several occasions to come off the goal line to intercept high crossballs and through passes.

By halftime, the score was 1-0 in Suriname's favor. We were lucky it wasn't 4-0. My coach, Conrad Braithwaite, took me aside during halftime and said, "Son, a jersey does not make a goalkeeper. You have not changed, only the jersey. You are still, by far, the best goalkeeper in this country." This was a turning point for me — not only because of what he said, but because of the way he handled the situation. He took me off into a corner, placed his arm around my shoulder and in a convincing, reassuring manner reminded me that I was a competent goalkeeper and that nothing had changed — the problem was all in my mind. I was fortunate to have had an experienced coach in my corner who was able to recognize my problem and the basis of my mistakes. By the second half, I was back to my old self again, and Trinidad and Tobago won its first World Cup qualifying game, 4-1. I learned three things as a result of that experience: always carry an alternate jersey or two, be aware of laws that affect goalkeeping equipment, and become accustomed to wearing different colored jerseys in game situations to avoid superstition as much as possible.

Fouls

The Shoulder Charge

While in possession of the ball or attempting to play the ball outside the goal area, the goalkeeper may be charged by an opponent legally, as long as contact is made shoulder to shoulder. In the United States, goalkeepers are overprotected to the extent that, nine out of ten times when a player legally charges a goalkeeper outside the goal area, a foul will be called and the referee will show a yellow card. American goalkeepers should be aware of this shoulder charge law, especially if they intend to participate in international competition.

The Four Step Rule

This rule is designed to stop goalkeepers from wasting time when in possession of the ball. The rule states that the goalkeeper can take up to four steps before releasing the ball. If the goalkeeper takes more than four steps while in possession of the ball, the referee may call an infringement of the four step rule and award an indirect free kick.

In game situations if a goalkeeper is off balance after catching the ball and uses six or seven steps to regain his balance, the referee shall not call infringement of the four step rule. Once the goalkeeper rolls the ball on the ground, he cannot pick it up with his hands until it has been touched by a player outside the penalty area. (He can, however, play the ball with his feet.) If the ball is handled by the goalkeeper after he rolls it on the ground, the referee shall call an indirect free kick against the goalkeeper.

Legal Challenges To The Goalkeeper

All goalkeepers must understand that an opponent has the right to stand wherever he chooses, including in front of the goalkeeper. When the goalkeepr is in possession of the ball and an opponent stands in front of him, he should not allow an opponent's presence to annoy him. Instead, he should do one of two things: throw the ball, or step to the side around the player and kick the ball. A smart opponent, if he detects that the goalkeeper favors one foot, will stand to the goalkeeper's stronger side, giving him space to kick only with the weaker foot. Therefore, goalkeepers should learn to kick with either foot. A goalkeeper who does not attempt to distribute the ball when confronted by an attacker can be called for delay of game (an indirect free kick). Conversely, a foul can be called against an attacker who interferes or attempts to interfere with the goalkeeper's distribution of the ball.

Free Kicks

There are two types of free kicks: direct and indirect. The goalkeeper must know the difference. He should learn all the referee's hand signals and observe these signals after each infringement. If in doubt, ask the referee to clarify the type of kick awarded.

It is amazing how many players are unable to tell the difference between a direct or indirect free kick. One easy way to differentiate direct and indirect free kicks is to become familiar with the ten penal offenses punishable by a direct free kick. All other infractions result in indirect free kicks. It is worth noting here that not all defensive fouls committed within the penalty area result in a penalty kick. Many players believe this to be true, but it is not. The following should clear up any misunderstandings regarding free kicks.

Direct Free Kicks

The nine penal offenses punishable by direct free kicks are:

1. Infringements committed with the hands:
    a. Handling the ball;
    b. Pushing;
    c. Holding;
    d. Striking or attempting to strike an opponent.

2. Infringements committed with the body:
    a. Pushing;
    b. Charging in a violent or dangerous manner.

3. Infringements committed with the lower extremities:
    a. Tripping;
    b. Kicking or attempting to kick an opponent;
    c. Jumping in or tackling in a violent manner.

If any of these infringements occur, a direct free kick is the result and a goal can be scored directly from that kick. If a direct kick violation occurs inside the penalty area, a penalty kick is awarded. Note that the position of the ball has nothing to do with whether a penalty is awarded.

What matters is where the foul occurs. For example, if the ball has been cleared to the halfline and the goalkeeper decides to get even with an opponent standing in the penalty area by punching him, a penalty would be the correct call (providing the referee or linesman sees the infringement).

Indirect Free Kicks

All other infringements are punishable by an indirect free kick. The ball must be played from wherever the infringement occurs, unless the foul takes place within the goal area. In this case the referee will spot the ball at the closest position, outside the goal area, to where the infringement was committed. In order for a goal to be scored the resulting indirect kick must be touched by a second player teammate or opponent. If an indirect free kick enters the goal between the uprights and under the crossbar without touching a second player, the referee shall indicate "no goal" and restart the game with a goal kick.

Defenders must refrain from attempting to protect their goalkeeper by blocking, pushing or running into the path of an attacker. If any one of these infringements occurs in the penalty area, the referee may award an indirect free kick — for blocking — or a direct free kick (penalty) for pushing.

The Field of Play

Penalty Area

The goalkeeper should be concerned with all markings in and around the penalty area for the following reasons:

1. His privilege of handling the ball ceases outside the penalty area;
2. The penalty spot is helpful in selecting the correct angle in positional play; and
3. The penalty spot (12 yards to the goal line) and the goal area (6 yards from the goal line) are helpful in indicating how far the goalkeeper is from his goal line.

The penalty arc is not considered part of the penalty area. It only comes into play in penalty kick situations when all players (except the goalkeeper and the kicker) must stay outside the penalty area and no less than 10 yards from the ball.

Goal Area

Goal kicks must be taken from within the goal area, anywhere from the midpoint of the goal toward the side on which the ball left the field of play. The ball does not have to be placed precisely at the top corner of the goal area.

Penalty Kicks

FIFA Law XIV states that during a penalty kick, the goalkeeper must stand with both feet on the goal line, between the goalposts, until the ball is kicked. The goalkeeper is allowed to move his body and hands before the ball is kicked, as long as his feet remain stationary and on the goal line. If the shot is saved and the goalkeeper moves his feet or one of his teammates steps inside the penalty area (including the penalty arc) before the kick was taken, the referee shall award a rekick. If, under the same circumstances the goal is scored, it is allowed.

On the other hand, if the kick scores and a member of the attacking team infringes in the penalty area or arc, a rekick shall be awarded. If the shot misses the goal, a goal kick is awarded.

Ball In and Out of Bounds

The entire ball must go over the line, on the ground or in the air, to be out of bounds. It is the referee's and linemen's responsibility to be in a position to judge whether the ball is in or out of bounds. Always play until the whistle blows.

Offside

The offside law is one of the most complicated of all soccer laws. The goalkeeper must be familiar with this law. Misinterpretation could be disastrous. FIFA Law XI states that a player is offside when he has fewer than two defenders nearer to the goal line than the ball at the precise moment the ball is played, except when he:

a. Is in his own half of the field;
b. Receives the ball directly from a drop ball:
c. Receives the ball directly from a corner kick;
d. Receives the ball directly from a throw-in.

Some teams play the offside trap. However, this strategy can be dangerous. I have seen situations in games when defenders attempt to spring the offside trap, only to have the referee allow the play to continue. When a team plays the offside trap, the goalkeeper must understand that sooner or later it will backfire. He should be alert at all times, supporting the space behind his defense by patrolling to the top of the penalty area and cutting off through balls. Goalkeepers must possess a clear understanding of the current offside rule. An attacker may be in an offside position and not be judged offside if he is not seeking to gain an advantage.

The Back Pass Rule

This new rule has proved to be very effective in encouraging teams to play the ball forward. The rule simply states that if a teammate passes the ball back to the goalkeeper, the privilege the goalkeeper has of handling the ball is over. He has to play the ball with his feet. However, there are two exceptions when the goalkeeper can use his hands to field the ball when it is last played by a teammate:

1. When the defender attempts to clear a ball and it accidentally goes back to the goalkeeper.
2. If the defender plays the ball to the goalkeeper using his head to make the pass.

Chapter 11

Shot Stopping

The area between the uprights and below the crossbar might appear to be small to the spectator, but in fact it is 128 square feet — a tremendous amount of space for one player to cover.

The goalkeeper's main responsibility is to defend his goal against shots. Some travel at tremendous speeds curving and dipping viciously, while others are taken from different angles and distances. The goalkeeper must have the ability to offer appropriate responses to the varying types of shots taken at goal if he expects to be an effective shot stopper. The following are key ingredients to effective shot stopping:

1. Angle play
2. Timing
3. Balance
4. Rhythm

Angle Play

A goalkeeper confronted by an attacker about to shoot on goal must try to make the task of that attacking player as difficult as possible. To do this effectively the goalkeeper must position himself in front of the goal where he has an equal chance of saving shots placed to either side of his body, on the ground or in the air, and reduce the space into which the attacker can shoot.

Positioning

Figure 11-1 illustrates how the goalkeeper can arrive at the optimum position based on the position of the ball. Two lines (A and B) are drawn from the two uprights and meet at the ball. The third line (C) connects the two uprights thus forming a triangle. A dotted line is drawn from the center of the goal on the goal line to the ball. This dotted line is referred to as the bisector line because it divides the triangle formed by the lines at A, B, and C. The goalkeeper standing on the bisector line has an equal chance of saving a shot to either side of his body.

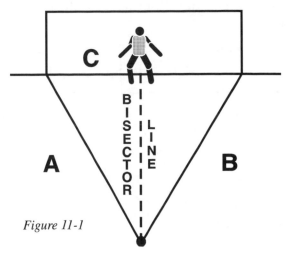

Figure 11-1

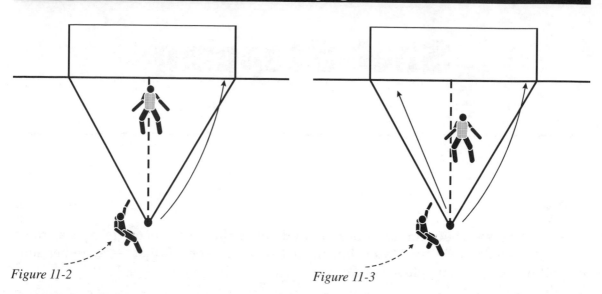

Figure 11-2

Figure 11-3

The position of the goalkeeper on the bisector line is only appropriate when the attacking player approaches from directly behind the ball. Whenever an attacker approaches the ball from an angle, the goalkeeper must make the necessary adjustments to his positioning in order to reduce the target space. Figure 11-2 shows the attacker approaching the ball from an angle and preparing to shoot with the right foot. If the goalkeeper positions himself on the bisector line the attacker can exploit the space to the left of the goalkeeper by curving the shot into the near post. Figure 11-3 illustrates the proper position of the goalkeeper. Note the position of the goalkeeper as he picks up a good position to the left of the bisector line. He is now in an optimum position to deal with the near post curving shot or a pullback shot to the far post.

Narrowing the Angle

Figure 11-4A shows the goalkeeper standing near the goal line at G1. At this position, the goalkeeper has given the attacker too much space to shoot into. As the goalkeeper moves down the bisector line toward the ball at G2, the target space on goal is reduced (Fig. 11-4B). The target space is further reduced as the goalkeeper moves from G2 to G3 (Fig. 11-4C). The goalkeeper must advance off the goal line and stay on his feet as long as possible in order to reduce the space on goal. This is referred to as "playing big."

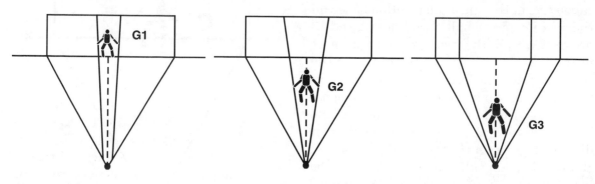

Figure 11-4A

Figure 11-4B

Figure 11-4C

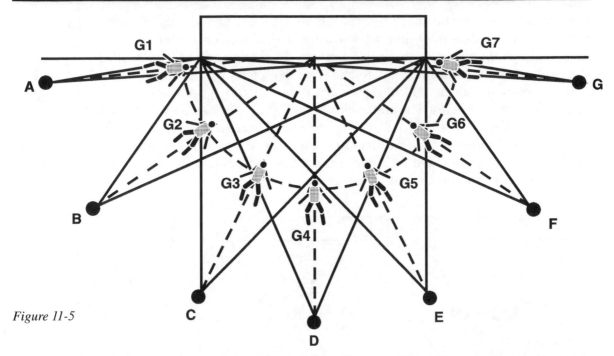

Figure 11-5

Figure 11-5 illustrates the positioning of the goalkeeper (G1 - G7) relative to the position of the ball (A-G). Note the position of the goalkeeper at G4 compared to that of G1, G2, G3, G5, G6, and G7. The goalkeeper at G4 is farther off his line than the others because shots taken from a central position provide the attacker with more target space to shoot into. The goalkeeper at G4, therefore, must move the farthest down the bisector line to reduce the target space. The more the ball moves toward the side of the goal the closer to the goal line the goalkeeper positions himself. Note the circular path of the goalkeeper as the ball travels from G1 through G7. At these two positions (G1 and G7) the goalkeeper is standing in front of the uprights, thus reducing the possibility of diving onto the posts.

Now that the goalkeeper has a better understanding of how to select the proper position for shots taken on goal, he must now learn to deal with these shots traveling away from his body. The selection of the appropriate diving angle is very crucial to effective shot stopping. The proper diving angle is formed when the goalkeeper dives across the path of the oncoming ball, as illustrated in Figures 11-6A and B. In Figure 11-6A, the goalkeeper makes a lateral dive. As a result of this lateral approach to the ball, the goalkeeper is able to get one hand behind the ball. However, in Figure 11-6B, the goalkeeper is in a much better position to make a two handed save by diving slightly forward. Note that the goalkeeper in Figure 11-6B narrows the angle by diving forward thus giving him the best chance of saving the ball cleanly. The goalkeeper in Figure 11-6A made a lateral dive and is able to get a touch of the ball with one hand thus conceding a corner kick at best. The goalkeeper in Figure 11-6C fails to narrow the angle with his backward dive and therefore has no chance of stopping the shot. Goalkeepers must be encouraged to dive forward when responding to low or high shots traveling away from the body because the forward dive narrows the angle and therefore reduces the target space into which an attacker can shoot. Goalkeepers must be discouraged from diving backward because this dive fails to narrow the angle, and therefore increases the space into which an attacker can shoot. There are three basic reasons why goalkeepers dive backward: (1) *Bad timing* — failure to recognize and anticipate when a shot is about to be taken. In this situation, the goalkeeper is not in the proper ready position to make the save. He picks up the flight of the ball too late and the response is usually a backward dive; (2) *Improper balance* — when a goalkeeper is on his heels and leaning backwards (Fig. 11-7) when a shot is taken, a backward dive is usually the result; (3) *Bending the knees toward the chest* — whenever a goalkeeper pulls his knees toward his chest on a low dive, before contact with the ball is made, the force generated by raising the knees will cause the top half of the body to move backward facing the goal (Fig. 11-8).

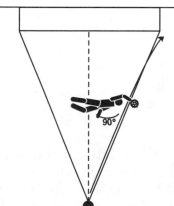
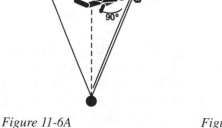

Figure 11-6A

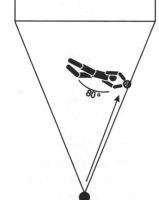

Figure 11-6B

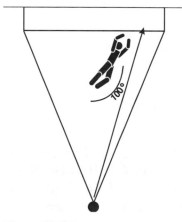

Figure 11-6C

Figure 11-7

Figure 11-8

Timing

The worst thing that can happen to a goalkeeper is to be caught unprepared, flat footed or moving at the moment an attacker gets off a shot on goal. Great goalscoring forwards (Pele, Muller, Cryuff, Rummenigge, Maradona, Grieves, etc.) all possess the knack of shooting when the goalkeeper is not completely prepared for the shot, i.e. when the goalkeeper expects the attacker to (a) dribble instead of shooting, or (b) the attacker gives the illusion of trapping, but shoots instead.

Quality goalkeepers must also possess the knack of knowing when an attacker is about to take a shot, and must respond appropriately by getting into the ready position. This is referred to as timing the shot.

Balance

Balance refers to the stationary position a goalkeeper adopts at the precise moment a shot is taken. When an attacker is about to take a shot on goal, the goalkeeper should cease his forward movement and ensure that his feet are comfortably apart and parallel to each other, the top half of the body is leaning forward, and the hands are held at the side and slightly in front of the body (Fig. 11-9)

Figure 11-9

Rhythm

Rhythm is a sequence of movements. Shooting rhythm is the sequence of movements generated by an attacker from the moment he decides to shoot (Fig. 11-10A) until the time the shot is taken (Fig. 11-10D). Goalkeeping rhythm is the sequence of movements made by the goalkeeper in response to an attacker's initial decision to shoot until the time the shot is saved (Fig. 11A-11E). Quality goalkeepers possess good goalkeeping rhythm. Good goalkeeping rhythm makes the difference between a shot deflected around the upright (a save) or a shot deflected inside the upright (a goal); a clean catch in the upper corner of the goal or a deflection for a corner kick.

Whenever an attacker is about to take a shot on goal, the goalkeeper must position himself so that he has the best possible chance of making the save. In Figure 11-10A, the attacker is getting ready to take a shot on goal. He steps toward the ball (with all the telltale signs that tell you he is going to take a shot), with his left foot.

The goalkeeper should mirror the attacker's movement by being positive and stepping forward to attack the ball (Fig. 11-11A).

The attacker in Figure 11-10B pulls his foot backward to shoot. Simultaneously, the goalkeeper hops off the ground (Fig. 11-11B) to prepare himself for a good, balanced position.

As the attacker makes contact with the ball (Fig. 11-10C), the goalkeeper lands into the proper set position (Fig. 11-11C). As soon as the ball leaves the attackers kicking

Figure 11-10A

Figure 11-11A

Figure 11-10B

Figure 11-11B

Figure 11-10C

Figure 11-11C

Figure 11-10D

Figure 11-11D

foot, (Fig. 11-10D), the goalkeeper picks up the direction the ball is traveling into and makes a step forward and sideways (Fig. 11-11D). The goalkeeper is now in an optimum position to take-off. In Figure 11-11E the goalkeeper flies through the air and makes the save. He them terminates his rhythm by landing (Fig. 11-11F) safely with the ball in his possession.

Goalkeeping rhythm varies from goalkeeper to goalkeeper. Coaches must understand this and make adjustments according to the goalkeeper's abilities. For example, if the goalkeeper has very sharp reflexes and is quite agile, he may want to follow the goalkeeping rhythm illustrated in Figures 11-11A through 11-11F. However, if the goalkeeper is a bit slow, he may want to make his hop (Fig. 11-11B) a bit earlier. Goalkeepers must be urged to work hard until they eventually come up with a rhythm that suits them best.

Figure 11-11E

Figure 11-11F

Shot stopping is the main defensive responsibility of the goalkeeper. In order for him to achieve quality goalkeeper status, he must master positioning (angle play), timing and goalkeeping rhythm. Goalkeepers must be trained often in situations where they are exposed to exercises which challenge them to master the arts of positioning, timing and rhythm. Here are two such exercises:

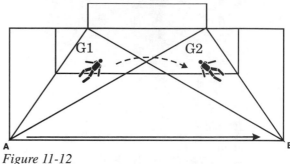

1. In Figure 11-12 two players are positioned in front of the goal, A at the inside left position and B at the inside right position. Because A is in possession of the ball the goalkeeper at G1 must establish an appropriate position in case A decides to shoot on goal. Instead, A passes the ball across the goal to B. The goalkeeper takes the shortest route across the goal and

Figure 11-12

then moves down the bisector line (G2) in preparation for the shot on goal. After the shot B passes to A forcing the goalkeeper to again move quickly across the goal to save a shot from the inside left position. In Figure 11-13A the attacker is about to take a shot from the center of the goal. At this point the goalkeeper is able to use the penalty spot to help him select the optimum position to make a save. However, when the shot is taken from the side of the goal —inside right or left — the goalkeeper has no point of reference he can depend on to guide him to the best position. As in Figure 11-13B, he may select a position which leaves the far post wide open or position himself leaving too much space on the near post (Fig. 11-13C).

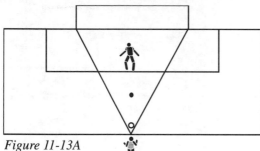

Figure 11-13A

2. In Figure 11-14, seven players are positioned in front of the goal. Each player has a ball and is assigned a number between 1-7. When the coach calls a number — usually in sequence (1-7) — the player takes a shot on goal. After saving a shot from player No. 1, the goalkeeper has to sprint across his goal and select the proper position (angle) to save shots taken by numbers 2, 3, 4, 5, 6, and 7. This exercise is invaluable in training the goalkeeper to select correct angles, improve timing and rhythm in a game-like situation.

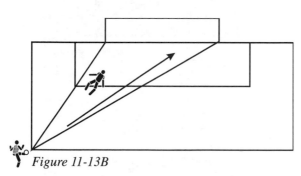

Figure 11-13B

The jugs machine or any other device that propels balls toward the goal is usually a useful training aid if used properly. However, these machines are not recommended for training sessions where timing and rhythm are the main foci of development.

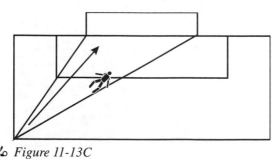

Figure 11-13C

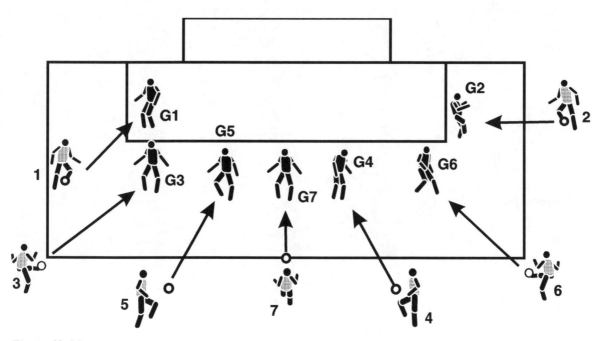

Figure 11-14

Chapter 12

Moving Off The Goal Line

Although shot stopping is a very important aspect of goalkeeping, proper timing in moving off the goal line to intercept dangerous through passes and menacing crossballs is the tactical quality that separates the outstanding goalkeeper from the mediocre one.

Intercepting Through Passes

There is nothing more frustrating to forwards than to see their accurate through passes intercepted by an alert goalkeeper. The goalkeeper who stays nailed to the goal line will find it difficult to intercept through passes.

The goalkeeper, being the last line of the defense, plays a role similar to that of a sweeper. He must be alert at all times, and position himself relative to the position of the ball. When defenders push upfield to maintain proper supporting distance behind the halfbacks, the goalkeeper must also push up to support the rearmost defender, even if it means being at the top of the penalty area. In fact, the modern trend among coaches is to encourage the goalkeeper to play well off his line and assume the new role of keeper-sweeper. This defensive tactic, although touted as being new, has been practiced by several goalkeepers in the past. In the late 60s, during my goalkeeping career, I can vividly remember the numerous occasions when I intercepted through passes as far as 20 yards outside of the penalty area. As a matter of fact, I can remember tackling players on two occasions as far out as 15 yards inside our own half of the field. The first one was in Guyana in an international championship series. Guyana was in possession of the ball on their right side and in their defensive third of the field. All our defenders were caught moving to the left anticipating a long pass down Guyana's right flank. Instead, the pass was switched over to Guyana's left flank for their overlapping fullback. Without hesitation, I sprinted out and won the tackle sending the ball into the stands and the player, Monty Hope, flying off the field.

The second time the scenario was identical, in a North American Soccer League final in 1970 between my team, the Washington Darts, and the Rochester Lancers. A long crossfield pass was made to the league's most dangerous forward, Carlos "Topolino" Meditteri. Carlos was well known in the league for his elusiveness and goal scoring prowess. We both reached the ball at the same time. He was able to touch the ball past my lunging tackle but was not quick enough to avoid a collision.

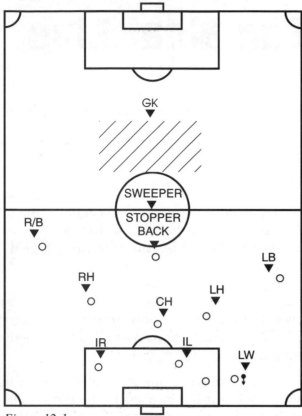

Figure 12-1

Although I was always criticized for my journeys outside the penalty area (the tactic was uncommon in those days) I can remember giving up a goal only once. This was against Birmingham of England. However, when I looked back over my goalkeeping career I realized why coming off the line and out of the penalty area came so naturally to me. For many years, at Division One level, I played at stopper — the last central defender in the third back system. Therefore, when I became a goalkeeper, my stopper skills added another dimension to my game.

I say all this to encourage coaches to allow their goalkeepers to play at sweeper whenever possible (scrimmages, practice, or exhibition games where nothing is at stake). It is very difficult to get a firm grasp of the keeper-sweeper role unless the goalkeeper gains experience at the sweeper position. It is unwise to force goalkeepers into a role which they are not capable of fulfilling. Natural ability, speed, agility, skills - outfield playing experience and ability to read the game all play a vital role in determining how far a goalkeeper should venture out of his penalty area.

The following are key factors to remember in moving off the goal line to intercept through passes:

- Always support the space behind the rearmost defender — keep the game compact (Fig. 12-1).
- Follow the game closely at all times.
- Anticipate long through passes, clever flick-ons (with the head), or wall passes intended for the space behind the defense.
- Come off the goal line when the pass is strong enough to penetrate the last line of defense.

1-on-1 Situations

Sometimes even the strongest defense is penetrated by a menacing through pass or by an attacker eluding the last defender with a creative dribbling maneuver, leaving the goalkeeper to face a 1-on-1 situation. This predicament is very difficult for the goalkeeper, and often results in a goal. With the proper training, however, a goalkeeper can change these odds drastically.

Preparing Goalkeepers to Face 1-on-1 Situations

The following coaching points can help goalkeepers learn how to deal with " 1-on-1."

Positioning — As mentioned in Chapter 1, the goalkeeper must position himself relative to the position of the ball and the rearmost defender (i.e., he must support the space behind the last defender).

Reading the Game — The goalkeeper must observe attacking players making runs toward goal and the behavior of the attacker in possession of the ball. In other words the goalkeeper must determine if the attacker with the ball is looking in the direction of a specific teammate making a through run. The goalkeeper must calculate whether the pass is moving quickly enough to beat the last line of defenders.

Confidence — Once the pass is delivered and it is obvious that no defender has a chance to win or tackle away the ball, the goalkeeper should move off the goal line quickly and with determination. He should have the attitude that he has a better chance to stop the attacker than the attacker has to score. All these factors determine the goalkeeper's readiness and will trigger a series of potential responses.

The goalkeeper should always be fully alert and ready to dash off the goal line to win the ball. The sooner a goalkeeper can judge the pace and flight of the ball, and whether the pass is accurate enough to beat the defenders, the better his chances of winning the ball. Inexperienced goalkeepers (especially those who have not been coached properly in dealing with the 1-on-1 situations) usually react after the ball has penetrated and is well into the space behind the defense. Needless to say the longer the goalkeeper takes to make his decision to come off his line, the less chance he has of being successful in 1-on-1 situations.

Variations of 1-on-1 Situations

Once the goalkeeper moves off the goal line in a 1-on-1 situation, he faces one of five possibilities. Methods of dealing with those five 1-on-1 situations are as follows:

1. Getting to the Ball before a Shot is Taken — The goalkeeper should approach the ball quickly, going to ground approximately 2-3 yards away from the ball and sliding toward it. The goalkeeper's approaching speed determines how far from the ball the goalkeeper must go down. As illustrated in Figure 12-2, the body is positioned on the ground behind the ball (like a wall) and is perpendicular to the oncoming player. The goalkeeper gathers the ball with the hands. Note that the head is kept as close to the ground as possible to avoid contact with the onrushing attacker.

Figure 12-2

Figure12-3

Figure 12-4

Figure 12-5

2. Arriving at the Same Time a Shot is Taken — The objective here is to smother the shot with the hands or the body and regain possession of the ball. If the goalkeeper is able to get his hands to the ball, he should position them behind the ball (Fig. 12-3). Although many goalkeepers have made successful saves using the feet first method, I strongly recommend using the hands first method for the following reasons: (a) a wider barrier is presented in front of the ball; and (b) the goalkeeper can see the ball, thereby increasing his chances of responding to the shot.

3. Arriving Just After a Shot is Taken (1-2 yards from the shooter) — The goalkeeper must get down to the ground as quickly as possible (to prevent the ball from going under the body) and slide forward (to reduce the space between him and the shooter) to form an effective barrier behind the ball (Fig. 12-4). Note the position of the hands and arms in front of the face and blocking the anticipated path of the shot. The head is held between the arms providing adequate vision and an additional barrier. The body faces the front. The grounded leg is positioned across the attacker while the upper leg is held high and bent slightly at the knee to block the shot should it pass that way.

4. After the Shot is Taken (2-3 Yards from the Shooter) — In this situation the goalkeeper must strive to minimize the space between himself and the shooter by diving forward. The forward dive must be low enough to avoid balls slipping under the body, yet high enough to protect against high rising shots (Fig. 12-5).

5. The Attacker is in Full Control — In this situation the goalkeeper must be prepared to deal with two possible developments: (a) the attacker shooting from short range (Fig. 12-6A); or (b) trying to dribble around him.

• Short Range Shot — When facing a short range shot situation, the goalkeeper should attempt to close down the space between himself and the attacker. He must challenge the attacker quickly but cautiously, with arms and hands held low and at the side of the body (Figs. 12-6 and 12-7) Ground shots from close range can be extremely difficult to save and the goalkeeper may be called upon to make a foot save.

- Timing The Short Range Shot — Stopping short range shots depends largely on the goalkeeper's ability to read the shooter's intentions. For instance by observing the attacker's running strides, the goalkeeper can predict when a shot is about to be taken. Usually, the strides of an attacking player — running with the ball toward goal — are of equal distance until he is about to shoot. The last stride before the shot is taken usually is longer than the others. Facial expressions, position of the non-kicking foot and tensing of the muscles are all telltale signs indicating that the attacker is about to shoot.

Figure12-6

Some outstanding attackers, however, are extremely clever and possess the ability to get off quick shots without telegraphing their intentions. Some of them also have the composure to fake shots causing the goalkeeper to go to ground, then they calmly dribble around or slide the ball past the fallen goalkeeper. Goalkeepers must develop the ability to read the attacker's intentions by observing the various telltale signs he may reveal during close range shooting situations. Goalkeepers should also try to stay on their feet as long as possible — Play Big — to avoid going to ground too early, thus leaving their goals wide open.

Figure 12-7

Figure 12-8A

Figure 12-8B

When the goalkeeper senses that the attacker is about to shoot (Fig. 12-8A), he must step forward and occupy the space between himself and the attacker. Just as the shot is taken (or maybe a fraction of a second before), the goalkeeper dives forward with his hands outstreched in front of him (Fig. 12-8B). His body is close to the ground to prevent the low shot from passing beneath him and yet high enough to deal with a rising shot.

- Attacker Attempting to Dribble Around the Goalkeeper — Some attackers delight in dribbling past goalkeepers and scoring in 1-on-1 situations. There are two ways a well trained goalkeeper can deal effectively with this type of player.

- Timing the Dribble Around the Goalkeeper — Some attackers delight in 1-on-1 situations. There are two ways a well-trained goalkeeper can deal effectively with this type of attacker.

1) In figure 12-9A, an attacker approaches the goalkeeper in a 1-on-1 situation. The goalkeeper approaches cautiously in preparation for a point blank shot. He very wisely stays on his feet until the attacker is about to play the ball with his right foot (Fig. 12-9B). The goalkeeper times the situation so that as soon as the ball is separated from the attacker (Fig. 12-9C), he pounces down quickly at the uprotected ball and comes up with a prized prossession — the ball (Fig. 12-9D).

2) The second way a goalkeeper can deal effectively with an attacker approaching in a 1-on-1 situation is to force the attacker into being a reactionary player. In order to accomplish this feat, the goalkeeper must have a basic understanding of attacking

Figure 12-9A

Figure 12-9B

Figure 12-9C

Figure 12-9D

players' behavior. Usually an experience attacker is trained (or possesses the ability) to exploit the goalkeeper's vulnerable points. For example, if the goalkeeper dives in feet first, the attacker will exploit the open or vulnerable side. If the goalkeeper approaches straight on and prepares to dive to his left, the attacker will tend to steer the ball or dribble to the opposite side. This reaction of the attacker in many situations holds true because he does not have much time to think, only to react to the goalkeeper's movements. A well-trained goalkeeper who is experienced in the way attackers behave in 1-on-1 situations can increase his percentage of saves by making the opponent become a reactionary player. In Figure 12-10A, the ball is separated from the attcker's feet. At this precise moment the goalkeeper steps quickly to the left and dives back into the space on the opposite side (Fig 12-10B). The attacker takes the fake and dribbles into what he thinks is the open space to the goalkeeper's right only to find the space occupied by the goalkeeper's body stretched fully across his path (Fig. 12-12C). I have used this fake tactic with great success against the likes of Pele, Terry Venables, and George Eastham, as well as in many World Cup, professional and international games. I must add at this point that this tactic worked well against skillful attackers who were well-known for their creativity and composure in front of the goal.

Figure 12-10A

Figure 12-10B

Figure 12-10C

I remember vividly the occasions when I tried this tactic and failed. The attackers never responded to my fake but instead reacted by shooting the ball powerfully past me. As a result of this experience I had to make several adjustments when faced with an attacker at close range. I would apply my fake-to-one-side tactic against a few of the skillful players in my country's (Trinidad) First Division league play and against top international players. I would change my tactic against lesser skilled players by staying on my feet and playing as big as possible hoping that they would shoot straight at me.

The point I am making here is that the 1-on-1 goalkeeping tactics mentioned in this chapter will never be 100% successful. Sometimes the goalkeeper can do everything right and still not prevent a goal. The goalkeeper must be prepared to make adjustments based on the opposition — which can change at any time.

It is important for the goalkeeper to select the right time to go to ground. If he dives too early, he gives the attacker an opportunity to shoot or dribble around him — exactly what well-coached attackers are taught to do. If he dives too late, then balls can go under his body or to the side of his legs. Proper timing is of the utmost importance in mastering the art of 1-on-1 situations.

Cutting Off High Crosses

A large percentage of goals are scored from high centering passes that cross the face of the goal. A competent goalkeeper reduces goal scoring opportunities by dealing effectively with such menacing crosses. However, that is easier said than done. Despite the fact that the goalkeeper has the legal right to handle the ball in the penalty area (giving him a big advantage), he is not always able to leap gracefully and collect high crosses without being jostled by oncoming forwards. In a crowded penalty area, even teammates can at times impede the goalkeeper's progress toward the ball.

Constant practice under match conditions is the only way a goalkeeper can master the skill of dealing with high crosses. Optimum performance can be attained only after the goalkeeper has developed good technique jumping to catch the high ball: explosive takeoff, rising with knee up to ward off incoming attackers, and catching the ball at the highest point of his jump or punching it to safety.

The following tactical points are critical to the goalkeeper's ability to "rule the airways":

- Positioning
- Judging the flight of the ball
- Deciding whether to move out, stay in place, punch, or catch
- Establishing a sound understanding with fellow defenders

Positioning

The position the goalkeeper adopts depends on the distance between the ball and the goal and the angle between the ball and the goal.

In Figure 12-11 the attacker A is positioned on the right flank near the goal line and approximately 5-6 yards from the sideline. He is preparing to make the most logical

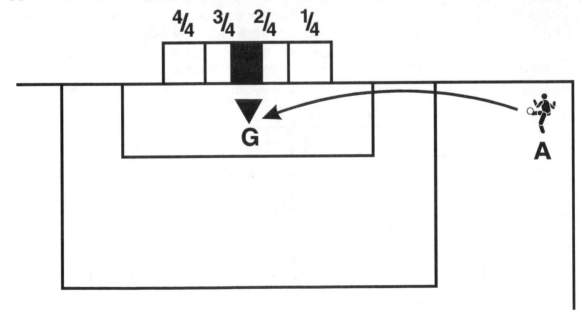

Figure 12-11

move, a right-footed centering pass across the goal. The goalkeeper should take a position near the center of the goal and approximately 3-4 yards off the goal line. The goalkeeper's height, quickness and leaping ability will ultimately determine which part of the goal he must cover. Given A's position on the right flank, and that he is about to center the ball with the right foot, the chances of the cross beating the goalkeeper at the near post are remote. Therefore, the goalkeeper is now in a good position to deal with either a near or far post center. If the attacker switches the ball from the right foot to the left, the goalkeeper should adjust his position and move closer to the near post (Fig. 12-12). He should be approximately 3 yards from the upright and 2-3 yards off the goal line in order to deal effectively with threatening inswinging crosses to the near post.

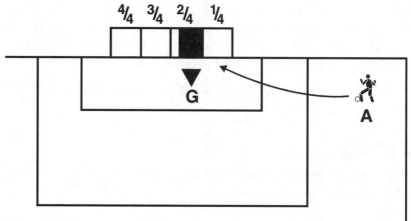

Figure 12-12

In Figure 12-15 the attacker, A, is now close to the penalty area, and preparing to cross with the right foot. The goalkeeper now has to slide down to the first quarter of the goal. If he comes all the way to the near post, he leaves the far post open and if he stays in the second quarter of the goal, the near post area becomes vulnerable. In this position (first quarter of the goal), the goalkeeper has an equal chance of intercepting or blocking both near and far post crosses. If the attacker switches the ball to his left foot, the goalkeeper should hold his position but be alert for an inswinging center to the near post or a curving cross to the far post. In Figure 12-14 the attacker A is positioned well inside the penalty area, approximately 12 yards from the near post.

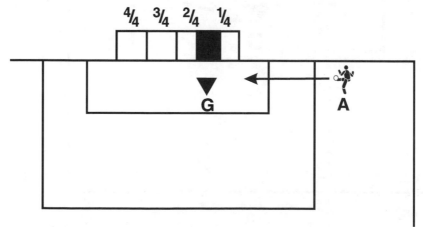

Figure 12-13

The goalkeeper must now move to cover the near post in preparation for a shot on goal, but he must also be ready to intercept, punch, or deflect any centering pass coming across the goal between the near post and the six yard box.

It is erroneous to believe that a quality goalkeeper can always control crosses in the six yard box. In Figure 12-14 the goalkeeper is vulnerable to a far post center. He must, however, focus all of his attention on near post shots and crosses. But in order to reduce the chances of giving up a goal from the far post chip, the goalkeeper must do two things:

1. Before the ball is crossed (preparation) — Take a quick look to the far post area to see if an opponent is making a blind side run and shout for a defender to pick him up.
2. After the ball is crossed to the far post (reaction) — turn and sprint as quickly as possible across the face of the goal to cover any shot from the far post area.

As mentioned earlier positioning for high crosses varies somewhat from goalkeeper to goalkeeper. The determining factors are height, speed off the mark, quick feet, and jumping ability.

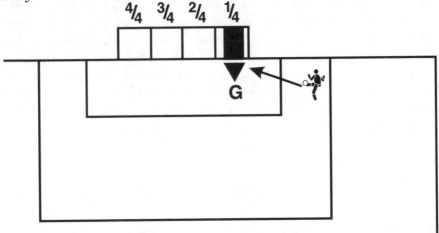

Figure 12-14

Judging the Flight of the Ball

Good judgment is crucial in dealing effectively with high crosses. The goalkeeper must be able to read the game and so anticipate and intercept high crosses. Many goalkeepers, even top World Cup netminders, encounter problems from time to time assessing the flight of the ball. One key to anticipating where the ball will travel is to watch closely to determine the kicker's intent. Is he preparing to cross the ball or shoot? Is he aiming at an open player? Moving toward the ball without first assessing its flight is the worst error a goalkeeper can make in a cross ball situation. This is the number one mistake in misjudging high crosses.

Deciding Whether to Move Off the Goal Line or Stay

Decision making in a cross ball situation is probably one of the most difficult goalkeeping skills to master. The pace of the ball, its line of flight and trajectory and the number of players between the goalkeeper and the ball must all be considered when deciding to move off the goal line or "stay home."

Any skill involving judgment is always very difficult to teach. The coach must expose the goalkeeper constantly to high cross situations — first with no opponents, then with opponents challenging for the ball, making the same type of contact with the goalkeeper as they would in a game, and finally with defenders as well as opponents challenging for the ball.

Once a goalkeeper has decided to leave the goal line, the move must be positive and aggressive. The goalkeeper must move decisively and quickly, keeping eyes fixed on the ball (Figs. 12-15A and 12-15B). There can be no hesitation, and no change of mind or uncertainty about reaching and controlling the ball. If in doubt the goalkeeper should "stay home" and take up a good position.

Takeoff comes with an explosive extension of the leg closest to the ball while the knee of the opposite leg is raised. While in the air, the goalkeeper should turn his body, without losing balance, to face the oncoming ball (Fig. 12-15C). The right leg offers protection from challenging players and the hands are positioned behind the ball. Again, the goalkeeper must concentrate on the ball and not allow oncoming forwards to distract his attention. Distractions, causing the goalkeeper to take his eyes off the ball, are a big danger in dealing with high crosses. Catch the ball at the highest point of the jump and bring it in against the body when it is safe to do so. When there is no one around, the goalkeeper can bring the ball down quickly against the body. However, when there are opposing players challenging for the ball in a crowded area, bringing the ball down quickly might cause the ball to be dislodged. In this situation, the goalkeeper should catch the ball at the highest point of his jump and keep the ball as high as possible above the players' heads until it is safe to bring it against the body.

Figure 12-15A

Figure 12-15B

Figure 12-15C

If defenders are in the way, the goalkeeper should keep his knee down to avoid injuring players. I have seen many goalkeepers wipe out their own players by coming off the goal line recklessly.

Establishing an Understanding with Defenders

It is very important that goalkeepers communicate effectively with defenders throughout the game, especially when they leave the goal line. As a goalkeeper I remember instructing my defenders before a corner kick or when a high cross appeared imminent, "If he lofts it, I'm going for it all the way." My defenders knew that once I yelled "keeper" they should get out of the way. There were often two defenders, and sometimes three, positioned on the goal line protecting the goal in my absence. They all knew that once I moved out, they should protect the goal. A positive goalkeeper leaves no doubt — among attackers as well as defenders — about his intentions. An early call lets everyone know where he stands.

Chapter 13

Back Passes To The Goalkeeper

When a defender is facing his own goal with an attacker in hot pursuit, he must pass the ball back to the goalkeeper. Such passes must be accurate and have the correct speed. An inaccurate or overly strong back pass can catch the goalkeeper off balance or unprepared, and the ball can go past him. If the back pass is too soft, an alert attacker might be able to step between the defender and the goalkeeper and steal the ball.

Although passing the ball back to the keeper might seem like a simple task, much work is necessary to ensure perfect coordination between defenders and the goalkeeper. I have been involved in several situations where simple back passes have caused considerable anxiety. Even at the World Cup level, misunderstandings between defenders and the goalkeeper have resulted in own goals. Especially with the new back pass rule coaches must spend quality time working with the defenders and the goalkeeper in order to improve their understanding in "pass back" situations. There are two ways a defender should pass the ball back to the goalkeeper: (1) to the feet and (2) to the space away from the goal. It is safer to pass the ball away from the goal for obvious safety reasons. The other benefit of passing the ball into the space away from the goal is that the goalkeeper is placed in a better position to clear the ball up the side of the field or kick it toward the sideline thus reducing the chances of a rebound goal. Nothing is more demoralizing in a game than an own goal. Some coaches and goalkeepers may prefer one method over the other, but whatever method is chosen must be practiced often so there is no doubt in anyone's mind. The following scenarios can help goalkeepers and defenders practice back passing.

Through Passes Intercepted by a Defender

The Situation

An attacker's through pass penetrates the defensive alignment. The goalkeeper moves off the goal line to intercept, only to find that a defensive teammate D has recovered and is in possession of the ball. The defender is now traveling with the ball, toward his own goal, with an attacker A on his back (Fig. 13-1A).

The Solution

The goalkeeper must analyze the situation and react quickly. He should recognize that his teammate is in possession of the ball, so there is no need to move further off the goal line. At this point the goalkeeper should stop and take up the basic ready position, thus offering the defender a standing target (Fig. 13-1B). At the same time he must inform the defender of the closeness of the attacking player. Such communications should be clear and simple — a shouted "Man on!" or "Behind you!", or any one or two words that would indicate to the defender that an attacker is on his back. The defender should respond by passing the ball back to the goalkeeper's feet or to space. It is important that the defender follows his pass.

This is a good habit to adopt because high grass or a wet field can slow the ball down enough for an alert attacker to intercept and score. After the goalkeeper receives the ball the defender veers off to the side to receive an outlet pass if necessary.

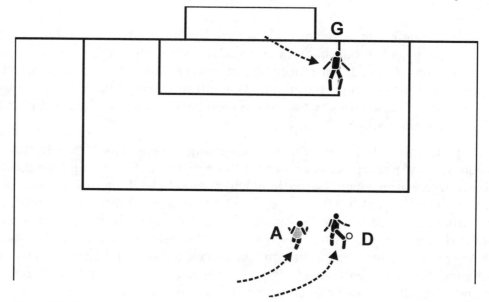

Figure 13-1A

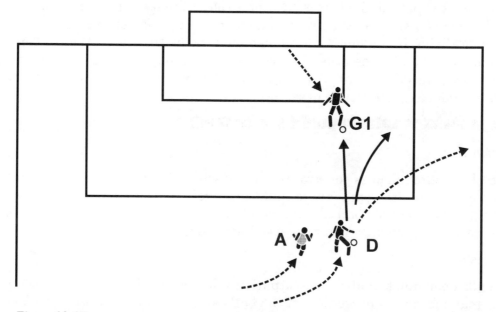

Figure 13-1B

Through Passes in Reach of the Goalkeeper

The Situation

The scenario is similar to that just described, but the goalkeeper realizes that he can get to the ball before the opponent D (Fig. 13-2A).

The Solution

The goalkeeper should let his teammate know that he is in full control of the situation (Fig. 13-2B) by shouting "Keeper" or "Leave, John" (or whatever the defender's name is), or any other command telling the defender in no uncertain terms, DO NOT TOUCH THE BALL. Misunderstandings in this situation can be catastrophic.

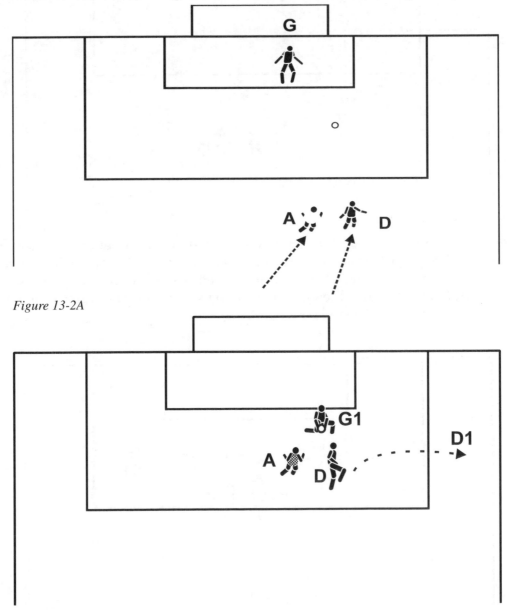

Figure 13-2A

Figure 13-2B

97

Through Passes Within Reach of Attacker

The Situation

The same situation as in situation 2, only the goalkeeper realizes that the attacker has a slight opportunity to get to the ball (Fig. 13-3A).

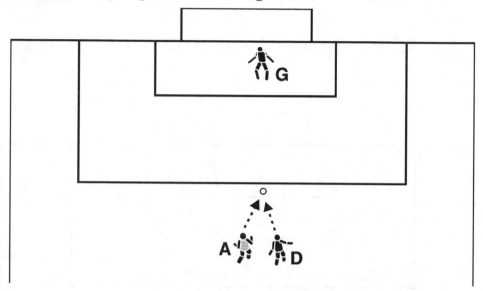

Figure 13-3A

The Solution

The goalkeeper must come off the goal line strong, shouting "Keeper." This command signals the defender to veer off to the right or left of the goalkeeper or jump over his grounded body. By positioning himself perpendicular to the oncoming players and the ground behind the ball, the goalkeeper is now prepared to get to the ball first or smother the ball should any player touch it (Fig. 13-3B).

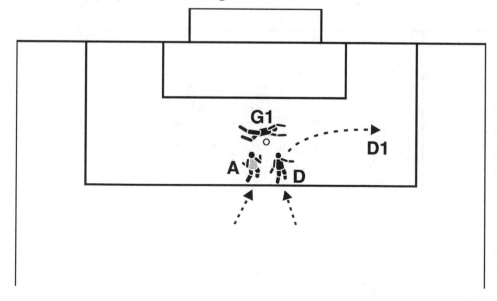

Figure 13-3B

In all these through ball situations, it is the goalkeeper's responsibility to make the call, not the defender's. This is mainly because the goalkeeper has the best view of the developing play.

On the day of the match, the goalkeeper must survey the penalty area and identify puddles, mud patches, or other field conditions that would affect back passing. He should point out these problems to the defenders and determine what tactics they should use during the game. The following are points to note when defenders practice passing back to the goalkeeper:

1. If there are puddles or mud spots in the penalty area, the goalkeeper calling for a back pass should take a position at the side of the affected areas. If there is no time for the goalkeeper to move to a clear area, the defender might elect to clear the ball sideways to the sideline for a throw-in.
2. After the defender plays the ball back to the goalkeeper, he should either follow the pass or run across the path of the nearest attacker, causing him to slow down momentarily. The defender must be careful, though, not to deliberately obstruct the offensive player in an effort to protect the goalkeeper. Obstruction can be called and the attacking team would be awarded an indirect free kick.
3. Defenders must respond spontaneously to the goalkeeper's call for the ball. The worst thing that can happen in goalmouth situations is for defenders to ignore the goalkeeper's instructions, either because they do not trust him, or because they are simply not accustomed to reacting to his commands. The latter is often true, because many coaches tend to train goalkeepers separately from the rest of the squad. Goalkeepers should be trained with the team as much as possible, especially in practice situations where teammates have the opportunity to respond to the goalkeeper's voice.

Supporting Angle

The Situation

In Figure 13-4A defender D is dribbling the ball up the left flank of the field. Opponents A and B move forward in an attempt to close down defender D.

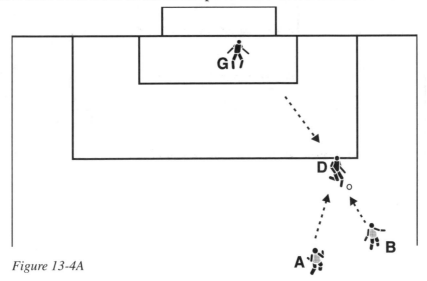

Figure 13-4A

Solution

An observant goalkeeper will recognize the problem his defending teammate is about to encounter long before the problem occurs. Furthermore, he will anticipate that turning back is the only option D has, and offer his support at the proper angle (Fig. 13-4B). Inexperienced goalkeepers tend to stay nailed on the goal line, therefore offering little or no support at all. If the goalkeeper stays on his goal line (Fig. 13-4C), it is very difficult for D to pull the ball back to him while under heavy pressure. In situations like this, when the angle is too acute, the defender D runs the risk of giving up a corner kick on his pass back if the support from the goalkeeper is not at the correct angle.

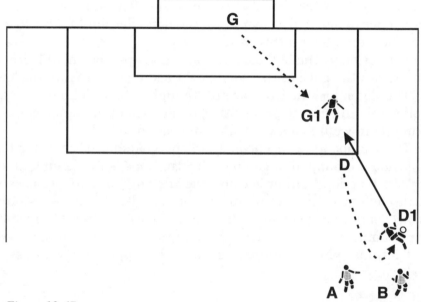

Figure 13-4B

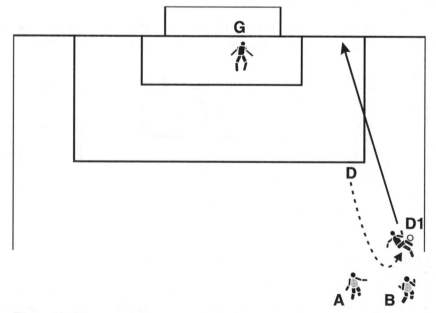

Figure 13-4C

The following exercise will improve communications between the goalkeeper and the outfield players. The exercise includes the outfield players, who are involved in interpassing, dribbling, tackling, ball control and positioning, and the goalkeeper, who is involved with all the skills that outfield players perform plus his own goalkeeping skills — catching and distribution. He is also able to control and direct teammates as the game progresses.

The game is called 3-v-3-v-3+1 (the goalkeeper). For example, three teams are selected, each team consisting of three players. Each team has a different color. One team becomes the defensive team, while the other two teams plus the goalkeeper (3+3+1) combine to keep the ball away from the defenders. The goalkeeper will always be on the attacking team. He has to play the ball with his feet. He can use his hands if the pass is lofted high.

In Figure 13-5A player A passes the ball to his teammate B. Player B is pressured on both sides by two defenders. The goalkeeper recognizes that his teammate (B is in trouble and needs help. The goalkeeper makes a good supporting run to G1 and receives an outlet pass from B, thus relieving the pressure. The goalkeeper is encouraged to loudly shout "Keeper!" when he wants the ball.

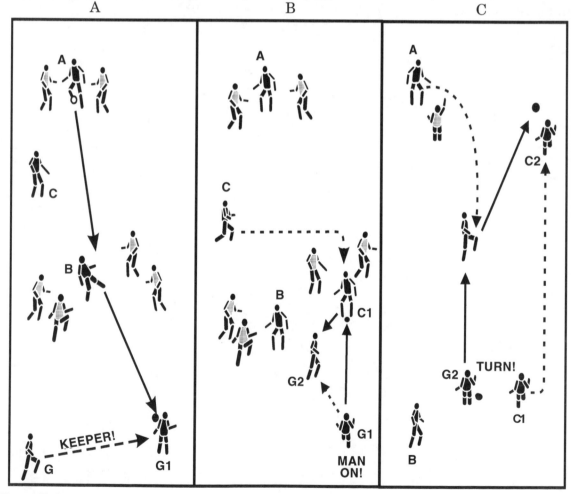

Figure 13-5

In Figure 13-5B the goalkeeper is in possession with the ball at his feet. Teammate C makes a forward run and shouts for the ball. He receives a pass from the goalkeeper at C^1. The goalkeeper recognizes that his teammate at C^1 is pressured, so he shouts, "Man on!" to warn his teammate of the defender who is about to place pressure on him.

The goalkeeper at the same time moves quickly into a new position at G^2 and receives a first time pass from C^1. The goalkeeper at G^2 (Fig. 13-5C) sees an unmarked teammate (+) and makes a quick pass. His command to teammate + is "Turn!" Player + turns and dribbles away to lay on a pass to an overlapping teammate at C^2.

Whenever a bad pass or trap is made causing the team to lose possession to the defending team, the player who commits the error will cause his team to become the new defending team.

This game can be played in an area of 60 x 40 yards. While this game is an excellent one for developing outfield players' endurance, patience in keeping possession of the ball and individual technique — passing, dribbling, ball control, tackling, etc. — it also affords the goalkeeper an excellent opportunity to practice supporting teammates and calling for the ball. Games of this sort are invaluable for helping the goalkeeper blend with the team and helping his teammates become accustomed to having the goalkeeper call for the ball.

Chapter 14

Restarts

Restarts account for more than 45% of the goals scored in World Cup and international soccer competition. This percentage is even higher in American soccer — particularly in college and high school play — because the playing fields are generally small (approximately 110 x 65 yards). This, coupled with the unevenness of many American playing surfaces, makes goal scoring from in and around the penalty area extremely difficult, increasing the dependence on restarts to score goals.

The goalkeeper, beyond stopping shots, has a tremendous responsibility organizing his defenders inside his team's defensive third of the field, the area 35 yards out from the goal line. He must ensure that his teammates are positioned strategically in order to deal with any attacking maneuver, especially on restarts. In order to deploy defenders effectively, the goalkeeper must (a) be aware of the vulnerable positions in front of the goal, (b) understand and be familiar with the various types of offensive decoy runs in free kicks and corner kicks, and (c) be able to assess the strengths and weaknesses of both defenders and attackers. He must ensure that each attacker is marked properly, (height for height, speed for speed) and that each attacker is matched properly (goalside and ballside).

Corner Kicks

The goalkeeper's position on a corner kick varies from person to person. The most orthodox or acceptable position is approximately 1-2 yards off the goal line, slightly beyond the middle of the goal toward the far post (Fig. 14-1). The goalkeeper should stand side-on so that he can see the kicker, the flight of the ball, and as many players as possible in and around the penalty area — especially those attackers lurking around the far post.

Some goalkeepers prefer to stand near the goal line, toward the center of the goal, when a corner kick is

Figure 14-1

taken, while others stand as much as 3-4 yards off the goal line. The position adopted depends on both the type of service — for instance, a right-sided corner taken with the right foot (outswinger) or the left foot (inswinger) and the goalkeeper's physical attributes (height, speed off the mark, and leaping ability).

The goalkeeper should be prepared to make adjustments based on his own physical attributes, opponents, type of service and field conditions.

It would be unwise to specify a "best" position for a goalkeeper to adopt on corner kicks. Whatever position is comfortable — and works — for the individual goalkeeper is correct. Personally, I prefer standing at the far post area 1-2 yards off the goal line for a right-footed corner kick from the right side of the field (Fig. 14-2A). For an inswinging left foot corner, I would slide down a couple of yards toward the center of the goal (Fig. 14-2B).

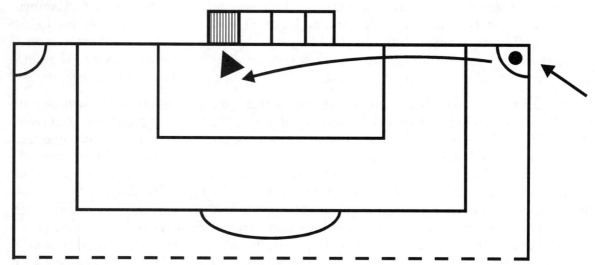

Figure 14-2A

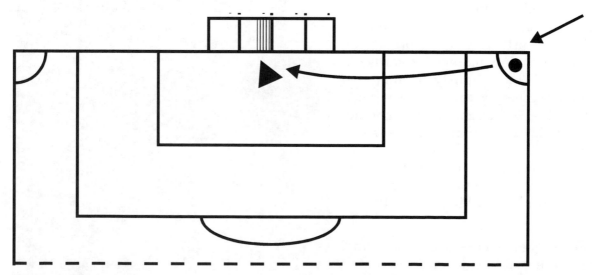

Figure 14-2B

Deployment of Defensive Players

In order to reduce goal scoring possibilities on corner kicks, the goalkeeper must be cognizant of the vulnerable positions in front of the goal (Fig. 14-2C), especially those at the near and far posts. He must be aware of the danger that accompanies each service.

The strategic deployment of defenders in and around the penalty area will minimize goalscoring possibilities during a corner kick. The three most commonly used types of defensive coverage are (1) zone or space marking, (2) man-to-man marking, and (3) zone plus man-to-man marking. Each of these defensive strategies has been used successfully by many top teams in the world. The best alignment in any given situation depends on the abilities of both defensive and attacking players. During my recent travels in Europe, I observed several club teams in Germany that preferred strict man-to-man coverage, and many English and Scottish teams that swore by zone marking.

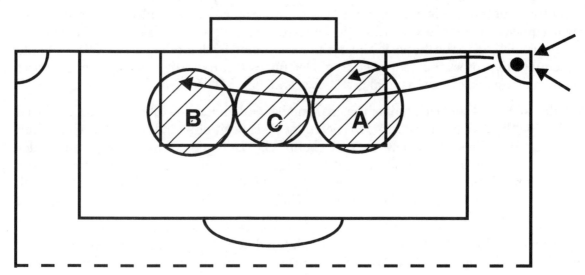

Figure 14-2C

Zone Coverage

In zone coverage all players are responsible for marking a particular area (zone) in and around the penalty area. In Figure 14-3A defensive player D^1 is positioned at the near post. His job is to attack and win any ball served into the near post area. Another defender, D^2, is positioned at the far post. His job is to protect the goal against balls lofted to the far post area. These two defenders also provide double coverage on the goal line when a shot is taken on goal by a second attacker from a corner kick (Fig. 14-3B) or if the goalkeeper moves off his goal line to intercept a high cross (Fig. 14-3C). In figure 14-3D a third defender, D^3, is positioned 10 yards from the ball. His job is to prevent the kicker from serving low hard shots to the near post area. In order to do his job effectively, defender D^3 must select a position based on the kicker's angle of approach and selected kicking foot. For example attacker A taking the corner kick is about to use his left foot from the right side of the field. Defender D^3 moves a few yards off the goal line in order to get in line with the flight of the ball. If the corner kick is taken by attacker B with the right foot, D^3 will take up a position near the goal line and in line with the flight of the ball.

In Figure 14-4A another space marking defender D^4 is positioned at the corner of the goal box area. His role is similar to that of defender D^1. Both must be aggressive and capable of sprinting forward to win balls served into the near post area. Defender D^5 is positioned inside the goal area and aligned vertically with the front half of the goal. His job is to support the space behind D^4. He must be one of his team's best headers of the ball. It does not matter whether he is a defender, halfback or striker. He must also be able to sprint forward quickly to deny any attacker the opportunity to score with a near post header or a dangerous flick-on to the far post. The positions occupied by defenders D^1, D^3, D^4, D^5 should be adequate to protect the near post area. Defender D^3 can further solidify the near post area by moving back near the goal area between D^1 and D^4 (Fig. 14-4B).

In order to defend the back half of the goal and beyond, defenders D^6 and D^7 are deployed just outside the goal area (Fig. 14-4C). Defender D^6 is positioned in line with the rear half of the goal. His role is to support the space behind D^5. Defender D^6 must be a good header of the ball. Defender D^7 is positioned at the edge of the goal area and must protect the space in front of and behind him. The defender at D^7 must also be a good header of the ball. In Figure 14-4D defenders D^8, D^9 and D^{10} seal off the space between the penalty spot and the top of the penalty area.

Figure 14-4E illustrates the deployment of all ten defensive players plus the goalkeeper. Defenders D^3 through D^{10} may have to adjust their position a yard or two toward or away from the goal based on the type of service or the direction the wind is blowing in relation to the goal. Figure 14-4F illustrates the seven most commonly used corner kicks in a game situation. There is a defender positioned to deal with each of the seven services adequately.

Some coaches prefer to use all 10 field players to defend on corners, while some prefer to defend with nine players and leave one at the half line for a counterattack. If the team wants to place one player on offense, D^9 is the most appropriate choice.

The defending team should also be ready to deal with an attacking team's decision to use a short corner (Fig. 14-4G). The kick is about to be taken by attacker A. His teammate, B, positions himself approximately one yard from the ball. Defender D^3

Figure 14-3A

Figure 14-3B

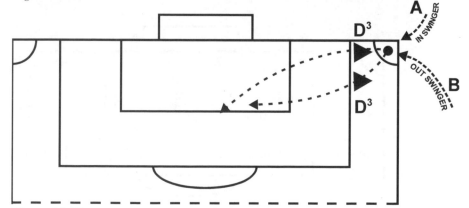

Figure 14-3C

Figure 14-3D

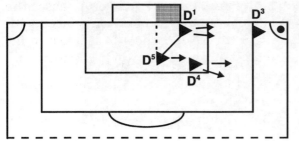

Figure 14-4A

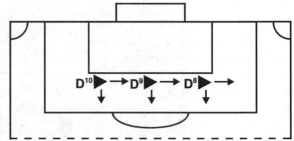

Figure 14-4B

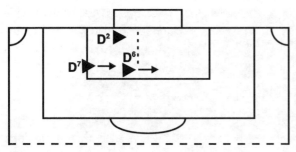

Figure 14-4C

Figure 14-4D

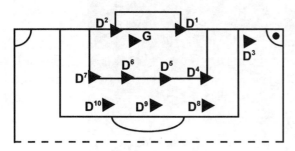

Figure 14-4E

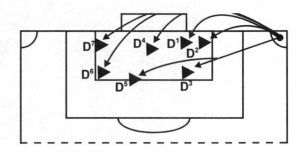

Figure 14-4F

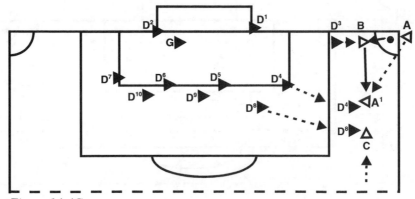

Figure 14-4G

must stay at least 10 yards from the ball until the pass is made. Player A passes the ball to B, who turns and confronts D^3 while A runs to A^1. At this point D^3 is faced with a 2 v. 1 situation. If B makes a lateral pass to A^1, A^1 can cross or shoot to the near or far post. A cross from this position is more dangerous than the conventional corner.

In order to neutralize this 2-on-1 situation, one defender must be designated to move quickly toward the area and create a 2-on-2 situation. The best choice for this task is the nearest defender, D^4. If an additional attacker, C, moves into the play, defender D^8 would be the appropriate equalizer for the defensive team.

Zone Plus Man-to-Man Coverage

If an attacking team has a player who is adept at scoring goals from corner kicks, the defensive team's coach might not want that dangerous attacker roaming around the penalty area unmarked. In such cases the defensive team's best header can be assigned to cover the attacking team's most dangerous player man-to-man while his teammates remain in the zonal coverage formation.

Man to-Man Coverage

Man-to-man marking is as the words imply: each attacking player must be covered closely by a defensive player. The goalkeeper must ensure that all attacking players are marked and matched appropriately, height for height, speed for speed. In Figure 14-5A the defending team is correctly aligned — man-to-man — and ready to deal with any type of direct corner kick. The defenders, with the exception of D^1 and D^2, are all marking their opponents both goal side (between the attackers and the goal) and ball side (approximately half a step ahead of their attackers). Note that in Figure 14-5B, several defensive players are marking their opponents incorrectly. Defenders D^3, D^4, D^7, D^8 and D^{10} are behind their opponents while D^5, D^6 and D^9 are parallel to their opponents. Both of these marking positions allow attacking players to get to the ball ahead of their defenders. It is imperative, therefore, that the goalkeeper remind his defensive teammates to mark up properly and cover their opponents goalside and ballside.

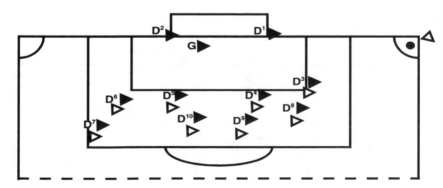

Figure 14-5A

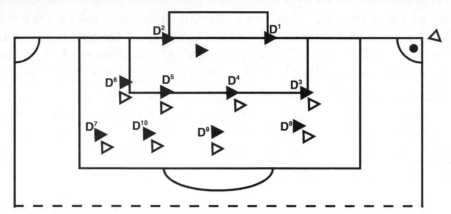

Figure 14-5B

Man-to-man coverage on short corners can be difficult. Which defender should be designated to neutralize the 2-on-1 situation created by the short corner? Figure 14-5C illustrates a short corner situation with the defending team marking man-to-man. Attacker B positions himself 1-2 yards from the ball. At this point the defending team must be aware that a short corner is about to be taken, and that a 2-on-1 situation is imminent. It would be risky for any defender to leave the player he is marking wide open in order to neutralize the short corner. The most appropriate defender to designate to neutralize this short corner is the defender at the near post, D^1. When D^1 moves out to assist D^3, the defender at the far post must slide down to guard the space at the near post (Fig. 14-5D) .

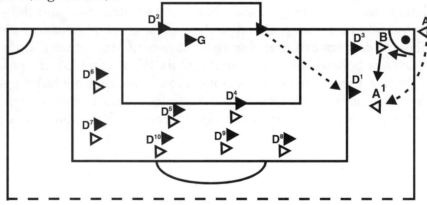

Figure 14-4C

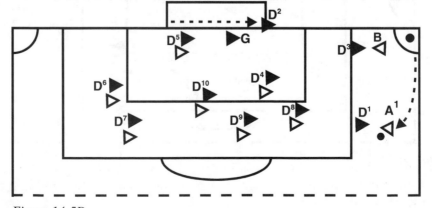

Figure 14-5D

Obviously, the far post will be left unguarded but this is the lesser of two evils — an unmarked attacker in the penalty area or an unmarked area at the far post.

Regardless of the type of defensive coverage a team decides to use in defending against corner kicks, the main ingredients for reducing goal scoring chances are:

- proper positioning — ball side and goal side
- each defender understanding his role and that of his teammates
- spontaneous reaction to the various types of corner kicks
- a determined attitude among defenders to attack and win the ball regardless of odds

Usually when goals are scored from corner kicks, the fault lies with a defender who has failed to fulfill his responsibilities — most of the time a forward or halfback who is not accustomed to winning the ball.

Free Kicks

The goalkeeper's two major responsibilities in defending against free kicks in and around the penalty area are:

- Ensuring that his defensive teammates are positioned strategically so they have a good chance to foil the attackers' attempts to score
- Positioning himself so that he can see the ball and has a good chance to deal effectively with shots on goal

Building a Wall

A wall is one of the most effective defensive strategies for dealing with free kicks close to the goal. Even so, a large proportion of goals are scored from set plays inside and around the penalty area.

When a wall must be set up, the goalkeeper is responsible for the following:

- Deciding whether the wall should be formed
- Determining the appropriate number of players in the wall
- Deciding who should be in the wall — forwards, halfbacks, etc.
- Directing the wall

When to Form a Wall

A wall is formed to protect the goal from a direct shot anywhere in or around the penalty area. Any free kick taken more than 35 yards from the goal line is unlikely to be a direct scoring threat. It is, therefore, poor tactics to set up a wall against free kicks from that distance unless the kicker has a reputation for scoring from more than 35 yards out, or there is a very strong breeze blowing toward the goal, or for some other good reason. However, one defender can be positioned in front of the ball to prevent the kicker from driving a low shot.

Number of Players in the Wall

The number of players in the wall depends on the angle from which the kick is taken. The figure 14-6A illustrates the various free kick positions on the field and the number of players in the wall for each.

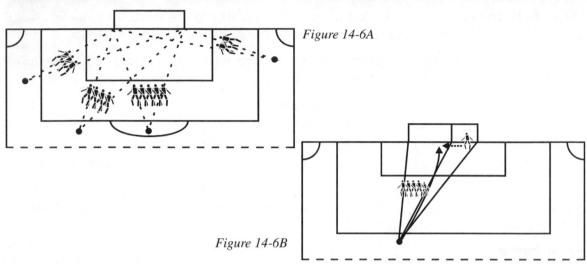

Figure 14-6A

Figure 14-6B

Free kicks from the center of the goal are always the most difficult to defend against. The shooter's angle is wider at this position, therefore more players must be pulled away from their defensive positions for the wall, increasing the numerical advantage for the attacking team.

Selection of Players for the Wall

The selection of players for the wall depends on the distance of the free kick from the goal. In free kicks just around the penalty area, the goalkeeper can expect a direct shot over or around the wall. Shots over the wall are the goalkeeper's biggest problem. In this case the tallest players must be deployed in the wall to reduce the over-the-wall shot on goal. On the other hand, if a free kick is taken 15-20 yards outside the area, the immediate threat is not a shot over the wall. Therefore, there is no need to place tall defenders in the wall. The attacking team will most likely opt to lob a high cross behind the wall. The taller players on the defensive team should be deployed to mark up and challenge for the high balls.

When wall players have been selected (preferably before the game), care must be taken to arrange them by height. In Figure 14-6B the wall is set up with the tallest player on the outside (toward the near post) and the shortest on the inside (nearest the goalkeeper). Should the kicker try to exploit the space over the head of the shortest player in the wall, the goalkeeper will have a better chance to save the shot than he would in the situation depicted in Figure 14-6C, in which the shortest player is positioned on the near post. Obviously, the rule should be the tallest at the near post and the shortest at the far post.

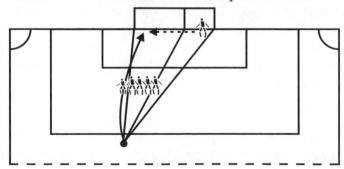

Figure 14-6C

Setting Up and Directing the Wall

It is the goalkeeper's responsibility to set up and direct the wall. I feel very strongly about this. As a goalkeeper, I felt more comfortable setting up the wall myself. This way I knew which areas of the goal were vulnerable. I would not be as certain if the wall was set up by an outside player. Some coaches, however, argue against allowing the goalkeeper to set up the wall. They feel that:

- To set up a wall effectively, the goalkeeper must go to the near post and give directions, opening the space at the far post and leaving the goal vulnerable to the attacking team
- The goalkeeper should be allowed to concentrate fully on defending against shots on goal.

I would advise goalkeepers and coaches to become familiar with both the goalkeeper and outfield player wall setting methods, and decide which is most suitable for their situation.

Teams should practice setting up walls so that every player will react appropriately to any free kick situation in and around the penalty area. It must be established who is going to be the "anchorman" — first man in the wall at the near post. Some teams will use the right fullback as the anchorman if the free kick is on the right side of the field, and the left fullback if the free kick is on the left. In any case, the anchorman is usually a responsible defender. If the kick is in the middle of the field, then the first of the two designated anchormen to get to the spot where the infringement occurred fulfills the anchorman's role. Other teams rely on one responsible defender to set up the wall for all free kicks.

Setting the Wall (by the Goalkeeper)

If the goalkeeper is setting up the wall, he must stand at the near post. From this position, he lines up the anchorman's inside shoulder with the ball and the near post (Fig. 14-6D). The other players in the wall must fall in on the inside of the anchorman. When moving the wall, the goalkeeper should use loud, clear commands consisting of as few words as possible (i.e. right! left! forward! back!). The goalkeeper should also note that, when directing the wall to go left, he means his teammates' (in the wall) left, not the left of the attackers.

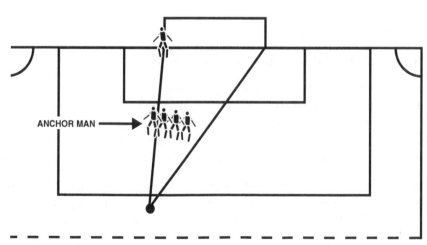

ANCHOR MAN →

Figure 14-6D

Setting the Wall (by an Outfield Player)

The wall can also be set up and directed by an outfield player, as illustrated in Figure 14-6E. The directing player should stand at least 10 yards behind the ball and line up the anchorman's inside shoulder with the ball and the near post. Using hand signals to direct the wall is appropriate since the players in the wall can see the director behind the ball.

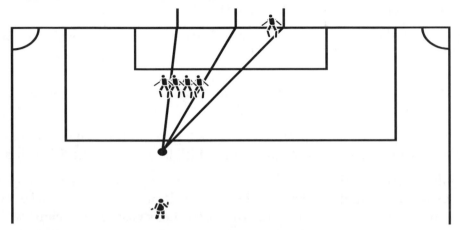

Figure 14-6E

Defending Against Different Types of Free Kicks

Although the wall is a very effective defensive strategy, it is still vulnerable. Some skillful players can bend shots around and over the wall. Teams with well rehearsed free kicks are also dangerous. In order to minimize the chances of conceding goals from free kicks near the goal, the defense, led by the goalkeeper, must be well organized and able to react instinctively at the moment a free kick is awarded. Obviously, good preparation in practice is essential. Each player must understand his function and be on the alert for deceptive decoy runs by attackers. Most of all, the goalkeeper must be aware of the vulnerable areas in front of the goal and of various types of free kick options the attacking team is most likely to execute. A goalkeeper who is able to anticipate attackers' intentions is more likely to make correct decisions and pass on useful information to his teammates. The following sections discuss the different types of free kicks usually executed by attacking teams.

Direct Over or Around the Wall

In Figure 14-7A, the player taking the free kick has the following options:

- To exploit the vulnerable part of the goal (the space behind the defensive wall) by chipping the ball over the top of the wall or around either end.
- To shoot powerfully into the part of the goal covered by the goalkeeper, hoping that the goalkeeper has, in anticipation of the ball being chipped over the wall, moved a little closer to the center of the goal(Fig. 14-7B), thus leaving the space on the far post open.

To defend against a direct shot, the goalkeeper must be alert and, while making a series of assumptions based on the attacking players' behavior, careful not to make premature decisions. The goalkeeper's position should give him an equal chance of saving either a chip over the top or a powerful shot to the near post (Fig. 14-7C). If the ball is chipped over the wall, the goalkeeper has a good chance of stopping it simply because of the length of time it must stay in the air. However, some skillful players possess the ability to kick the ball sharply over the top or around the wall. The goalkeeper must be aware of this and must work constantly on his foot speed to get him across the front of the goal quickly. If an opposing team has a player who is adept at scoring from free kick by serving the ball over and around the wall, I would position a defender on or near the goal line behind the wall and toward the near post (Fig. 14-7D).

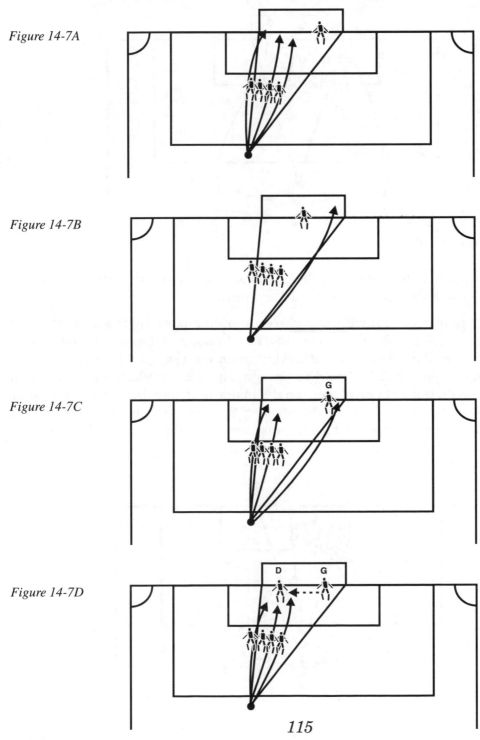

Figure 14-7A

Figure 14-7B

Figure 14-7C

Figure 14-7D

Short Lateral Pass Followed by a Shot

In Figure 14-8A the kicker, A, makes a quick short pass to his right, allowing team-mate B to shoot into the unprotected part of the goal at the far post. Player A could also pass the ball to the left for C to shoot into the goal at the near post. It is amazing how effective this simple type of free kick can be. This is mainly because most players in a wall have the tendency to hold their positions after the ball is played laterally.

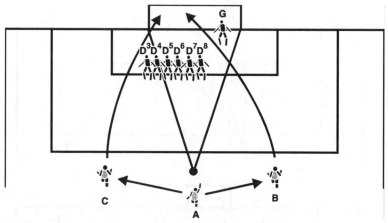

Figure 14-8A

To defend against the short free kick, the goalkeeper must remind the players that the wall becomes ineffective if the ball is passed laterally.

If the attacking team lines up with one player standing close by the kicker's right (Fig. 14-8B), the goalkeeper should anticipate a short pass and deploy a defender (D^1) to close down the possible pass. If the attacking team positions another player at C, then an additional defender (D^2) should be brought in to foil any attempts from that side. In the wall itself, the last two players on the inside of the wall (D^7 and D^8) must be prepared to break and move toward the shooter B. If the ball is passed to C, the anchorman D^3 and the player next to him D^4 must also move forward to foil C's chances of getting off a shot.

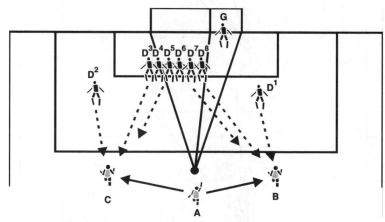

Figure 14-8B

A Forward Pass Followed by a Lateral Pass Then a Shot

In Figure 14-9A attacker F is positioned in front of the wall. Player A passes to F, who can make a first time lateral pass to either B or C for a shot on goal.

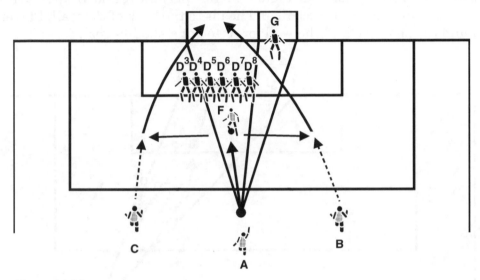

Figure 14-9A

To defend against the forward/lateral pass, the goalkeeper must ensure that all attacking players are marked. Close attention must be paid not only to the two attackers B and C, but also to F, who is standing in front of the wall. When the ball is passed to F, one of the players in the wall (D^8 if he is alert and reads the situation correctly) might be able to step forward and intercept or prevent the lateral pass.

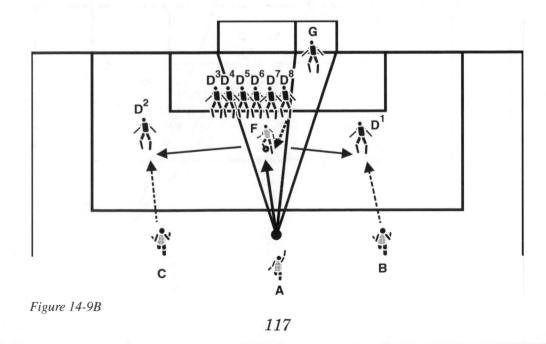

Figure 14-9B

117

Passes Made Into Space Behind the Wall

Over the Top of the Wall

This type of kick is usually attempted when there is enough space behind the wall for an attacker to receive a pass. In Figure 14-10A players A and B approach the ball. Player A runs over the top of the ball and heads to the back of the wall. Player B chips the ball into the space behind the wall for A¹ to get a shot on goal.

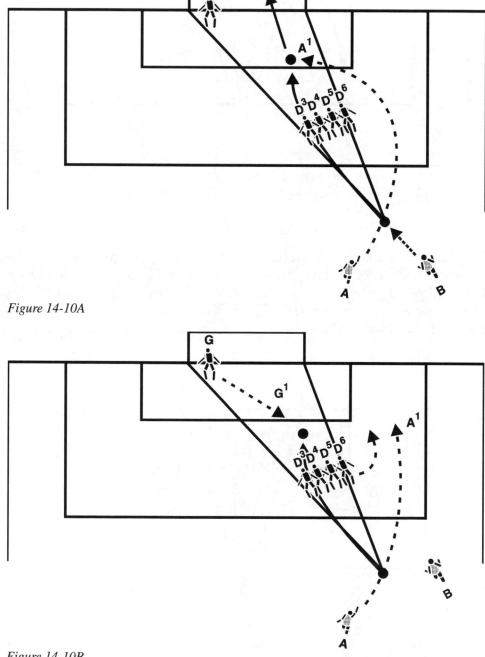

Figure 14-10A

Figure 14-10B

Around the Side of the Wall

Players A and B approach the ball. Player A runs over the top. The ball is passed to C who makes a first time pass behind the wall for A[1] to run onto and either shoot or go 1-on-1 with the goalkeeper (Fig. 14-11A).

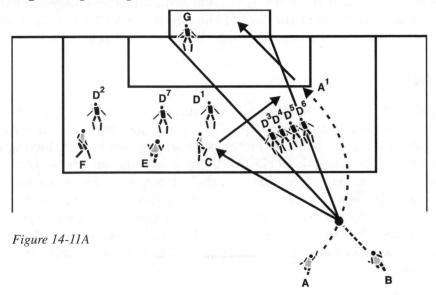

Figure 14-11A

To defend against these two types of free kicks, as shown in figures 14-10A and 14-11A, the goalkeeper must first read the clues that indicate such plays may be developing. The kicker's distance from the goal, attackers at the ends of the wall, or an attacker running toward the space behind the wall are all reliable indicators. When a chip appears likely, the goalkeeper must be prepared to move off the goal line to intercept. The defenders on either end of the wall must also be alert and prepared to step backward (once the ball is chipped over the wall) as in figures 14-10B and 14-11B, to contain any attackers who might attempt to run into the space behind the wall.

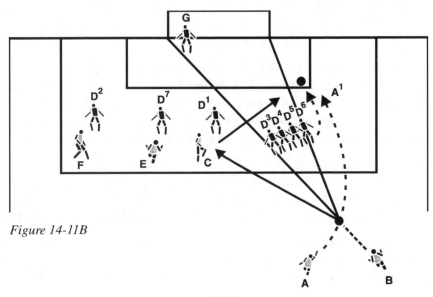

Figure 14-11B

It is virtually impossible to mention all the different types of free kick options outside the penalty area. However, I have found through my many years as a professional goalkeeper and coach that most free kicks near the goal are identical to or variations of the four types just described. It is most important to mention, however, that most free kicks taken near the goal involve several deceptive maneuvers before the ball is played. Therefore, the goalkeeper and the rest of the defensive unit must be alert for decoy runs and other actions that are designed to make them relax or misread an attacker's intentions.

Penalty Kicks

Saving penalty kicks is, first and foremost, a matter of positive mental attitude. Whenever I was faced with a penalty kick situation, there was no doubt in my mind that I would stop the ball. I knew that all the pressure was on the kicker (having been in his position on several occasions). Certainly there was none on me — if I stopped the penalty shot, I was a hero, receiving as much praise as an outside teammate who scored a goal. And if the kick scored, it was no reflection on me, because the probability of a penalty kick scoring is very high. Even after a score, if I had gotten my hands to the ball or even just chosen the correct corner, I would be complemented for my efforts. This attitude in penalty kick situations helped immensely to remove the pressure on me as a goalkeeper.

Looking back over my goalkeeping career, I can now appreciate and understand how I developed such a positive mental attitude toward penalty kick situations. I spent a tremendous amount of time, in practice and in competitive situations, stopping penalties in my early years of goalkeeping. I enjoyed having penalty kick contests with my teammates and used to challenge them regularly after practices. I would bet two or three of them that I would stop a minimum of 6 out of their 10 penalty kicks. The losers ended up buying the winners Cokes. These contests became quite popular (especially since I did most of the buying). After a while many players became interested in participating. In order to accommodate them, I would form two teams with a goalkeeper on each team. If there were three goalkeepers available, I would divide the players into three teams. The team allowing the fewest goals would be the winner. The players on the second and third teams would each buy a Coke for the members of the winning team.

These penalty kick contests provided a great deal of enjoyment for everyone who participated but, more importantly, they offered the goalkeepers the opportunity to practice stopping penalty kicks in a competitive and pressured environment. As a result of these contests I was able to develop a keen eye for where penalty kickers would be shooting, based on their approach to the ball and other telltale signs.

I cannot overemphasize how important it is to always make penalty kick situations competitive in practice. This competitiveness places pressure on kickers, sometimes causing them to miss the target because they are either too anxious to score or too scared of missing. In competitive situations, players tend to be more predictable.

If there is no competition (lack of pressure), they tend to try all sorts of shots, in all directions, just to deceive the goalkeeper. This makes it very difficult for the goalkeeper to develop a systematic approach to predicting the direction of penalty kicks.

Tendencies of Kickers

Most penalty kickers are quite predictable in the angle from which they approach, and ultimately from the position of the feet and body (leaning forward or backward prior to contact with the ball). Good scouting reports can provide the goalkeeper with valuable information regarding the tendencies of opposing teams' penalty kickers.

If the goalkeeper spends time carefully observing penalty kickers — not only in his own league but all over the world — he can soon develop a set of guidelines to help him predict the direction of a penalty kick. Quality goalkeepers are thinking goalkeepers, and as such, are always armed with a set of such theories to help them make sound decisions on the field.

Figure 14-12A shows the various angles from which a right-footed player can approach the ball for a penalty kick. The kicker who approaches the ball from position A will find it difficult to place the ball to the goalkeeper's left. He has two choices. He would have to kick across the ball with the outside of the instep (splice kick) as in Figure 14-12B. Or, during the last steps of his approach, he could place the nonkicking foot approximately 12-14 inches to the side of the ball, lean the upper body backward and away from the ball, and strike the ball with the inside of the foot (Fig. 14-12C). Without these alternatives in approach, the chances are very good that the ball will fly to the goalkeeper's right (Fig. 14-12D). Only twice in my 30 year career do I remember a right-footed player kicking the ball to my left off a direct approach. The first player was a fleet-footed striker in my country named Gwynwyn Cust. The game between his team, Colts, and my team, the Regiment, was always a doggedly fought one with the winner gaining no more than a one goal advantage. Gwynwyn approached the ball and executed a splice kick, sending the ball to my left while I went flying to the opposite corner. Although the game was tied at that particular time it took a great deal of composure to perform such a risky kick.

The second time was in an international game between Arsenal of England and Trinidad and Tobago in 1965. The kicker was George Eastham, at that time a member of the English national team. His approach was identical to Gwynwyn's, and the result was the same.

For a time, these two incidents made me question my ability to predict the path of penalty kicks, until I noticed on the video of the Arsenal game that George Eastham's feet were pronated — that is, that he was pigeon-toed. Players with pronated kicking feet can approach from directly behind the ball and execute a splice kick naturally because of the angle at which the foot is attached to their leg. However, the outside of the kicking foot is not commonly used because of the high risk that the shot will be kicked wide of the goal.

Since these two incidents no other player has taken that type of splice kick against me or one of my teams. The point I am making here is that goalkeepers should not abandon their theories too soon, but should allow enough time to see whether they work. Generally, players approaching the ball from position A and occasionally from position 1 (Fig. 14-12E), tend to kick to the goalkeeper's right.

If a kicker approaches from positions 2, C, 3 and places the nonkicking foot approximately 12-14 inches to the side of the ball, leans the upper body away from the ball, leans backward, and turns the kicking leg out from the hip, then he is likely to place

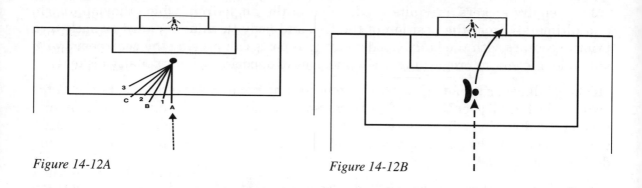

Figure 14-12A

Figure 14-12B

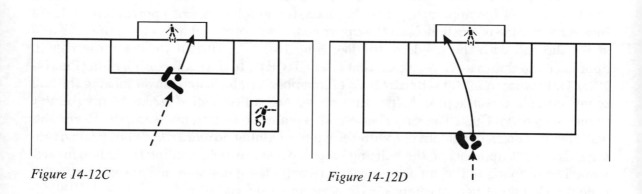

Figure 14-12C

Figure 14-12D

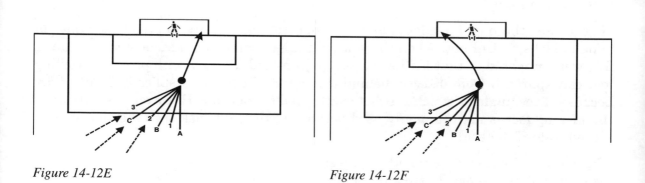

Figure 14-12E

Figure 14-12F

the ball to the goalkeeper's left (Fig. 14-12E). If he approaches from positions 2, C, 3, he also has the option of going to the goalkeeper's right without difficulty (Fig. 14-12F). This time the kicker places his nonkicking foot nearer to the ball (8-10 inches), and has a more upright stance on contact with the ball. Obviously, it is more difficult to detect the direction in which a penalty kick will travel when the kicker approaches from B, 2, C and 3, because he can very easily go both to the goalkeeper's left or right. Sometimes a player's nationality can be a helpful clue for the goalkeeper. From the late 1950s through the early 1970s, when I was playing at the international level, British players kicking with the right foot tended to place shots to the goalkeeper's left. Their rationale, or that of their coaches, was that since most goalkeepers were right-handed, they were presumably weaker on their left side. In addition, a shot to the left sends the ball curving away from the goalkeeper (Fig. 14-12E). South Americans, on the other hand, traditionally kicked their penalties across the goalkeeper's face (i.e. shoot with the right foot sending the ball to the goalkeeper's right — Fig. 14-12F). These penalty shots are easier to stop because they travel closer to the goalkeeper than those illustrated in figure 14-12E.

In modern soccer, however, styles of playing and penalty kicking have become more and more unpredictable since players are also opting to shoot straight down the middle of the goal.

Strategy for Saving Penalty Kicks (Regulation Time)

Most coaches select a player as the team's number one penalty kicker. Two alternates might be chosen for occasions when the number one kicker is injured or not having a good game. These players are usually the best penalty kickers on the team to begin with, and it is reasonable to assume that they might practice more frequently than the others placing penalty shots as close to the uprights as possible. Therefore, goalkeepers can expect penalty kicks during games to be taken by players who are confident, well-practiced, and consistent — that is, expected to place the ball near the uprights on nine out of ten tries. Very seldom does a player shoot down the middle of the goal when a penalty kick is awarded during a game. This usually occurs in penalty kick shoot-outs at the end of the game.

Goalkeepers can also presume that the kicker has only two options: to shoot to the left or right of the goalkeeper. In order to enhance the possibility of stopping penalty kicks during regulation time, the goalkeeper must adhere to the following:

a. Do your homework. Scout teams to find out how their penalty kickers generally place the ball.
b. Express confidence through your look and actions from the moment the penalty kick is awarded. This can be very unnerving to kickers. For instance, while the referee is clearing the penalty area in preparation for the kick, the goalkeeper might start jogging along the goal line or in front of the goal just to show the kicker that he must do a good job to get a shot in the net. I have done this on many occasions and have seen players change their minds as many as three times before taking the kick. *However, the goalkeeper must be careful not to confuse unsportsmanlike, disruptive antics with a show of confidence.*
c. Concentrate. Don't worry about whether the referee's call was a good one or not, about your teammates, or about anyone on the opposing team but the kicker. Focus all your attention and energy on stopping the shot. The situation is now 1-on-1, and

the psychological warfare has begun. Be prepared to either anticipate where the kicker will place the ball and dive into a predetermined corner as soon as he touches the ball, or hold your ground and not dive too early. Go after the ball as soon as the shot is taken.

d. Be alert for signals from the kicker. Sometimes, when a player spots the ball to take a penalty kick, he unconsciously glances into the corner into which he is about to shoot the ball. The goalkeeper must also be alert for such messages. The goalkeeper must also be careful not to let the kicker see that he has noticed him (the kicker) looking at the target. Clever players will trick the goalkeeper by looking into one corner and shooting to the other.

e. Check the kicker's position and approach to the ball (as illustrated in Figure 14-12A.)

f. Try to fake the kicker. Once the player is set to take the kick, and the goalkeeper has decided to dive to his own left, the goalkeeper must try to convince the kicker that he is going to dive in the opposite direction. This can be accomplished by leaning slightly to the right. Slightly is the key word here. If the goalkeeper leans too far to one side the smart penalty kicker might read the bluff and place the ball to the side to which the goalkeeper is leaning. Swaying from side to side sometimes sends false messages to the penalty kicker causing him to lose concentration.

g. Dive as soon as the kicker touches the ball. As the kicker's foot makes contact with the ball, the goalkeeper must dive forward and sideways toward the corner of his choice. Diving as soon as the player touches the ball gives the goalkeeper a split second more to cover the distance between himself and the upright. Diving forward brings the goalkeeper closer to the ball, narrowing the angle and enhancing the chances of getting a hand on the shot. Diving sideways, with the front of the body facing the ball, ensures that the goalkeeper's hands will be positioned behind the ball, giving him a better chance of deflecting the shot around the upright.

h. Some top level goalkeepers, for example Sheffield's United's Alan Hodgkinson during the latter stages of his career, choose to stand their ground until the kick is taken, then move to intercept.

Looking back over my career, I vividly remember utilizing the aforementioned techniques with a great deal of success. My theories were not always right, but they helped me develop confidence in penalty situations. I always believed that I had a great chance of stopping all penalties. The following penalty situations remain in my mind.

Chelsea of England v. Trinidad & Tobago (1964)

The kicker was Terry Venables — at that time, the starting striker for England — formerly head coach of Barcelona FC in Spain, and now manager of Tottenham Hotspur in the English First Division. Terry spotted the ball and I saw him glance briefly toward the corner on my left side. I turned my head away before he noticed me looking at him. As he moved back to his starting position, I dropped my right hand and leaned slightly to my right. He positioned himself approximately eight paces behind and three paces to the side of the ball (see Fig. 14-12A, position 2). Just as his foot made contact with the ball I went flying into the left corner and deflected the shot (that was placed inches from the upright) around the post. Terry confessed afterward that he saw me leaning to the right and felt for sure he had me fooled.

Arsenal v. Trinidad & Tobago (1965)

A penalty kick was awarded to Arsenal in the first half of the game. George Eastham was the kicker. His approach differed from Terry's. He positioned himself directly behind the ball (Fig. 14-12B at A). There was every indication that he was going to place the ball to my right (with his right foot). As his foot made contact with the ball, I went flying into the corner to my right only to see the ball spinning into the opposite corner. After the game, I asked him why he chose the corner he did. He said that I was leaning too much to my left, and therefore, gave myself away.

Guyana v. Trinidad & Tobago (1961)

The penalty kicker, Monty Hope, was very predictable. While spotting the ball, he looked into the corner where he intended to shoot, and his approach was from the side (Fig. 14-12A at position B). He shot to my left and I was there to deflect the ball around the post. The referee called a rekick because he thought I moved too soon. Monty adjusted his approach from the side of the ball to directly behind it. The shot was placed to my right and again I was there to deflect the ball, but again the referee called me for moving too soon.

By that time Monty's confidence was shattered so another kicker was chosen. I was totally convinced that, after seeing me stop the two previous kicks, this new kicker must be nervous. So I smiled confidently at him. The shot was taken and flew harmlessly high and wide of the goal. At a reception that evening, he told me that he had planned to place the ball to my right but my smile threw him off completely, so he changed his mind — while running up to the ball — and decided to kick the ball powerfully.

An important word of advice. Don't treat your competitors as your enemy, always talk to them after the game or soon thereafter. The information they can share with you is invaluable.

Tiebreaker Shootouts

Tiebreaker penalty kick shootouts, which can consist of five or more penalty kicks, pose a greater challenge to even the most experienced players — kickers *and* goalkeepers. The pressure is greater because the game can be decided on any one of these kicks. At least in regulation time if a player misses a penalty kick, he might still have some time during the game to redeem himself. In a shootout if he misses, it's all over. For this particular reason the tendencies of penalty kickers are somewhat different from those of players kicking during regulation time.

Over the years I have been privileged to experience tiebreaker situations from three perspectives: that of a goalkeeper, penalty kicker and coach. As a result, I have formulated several different theories on stopping penalty kicks, but there is one theory which served me best over the years.

When faced with a tiebreaker penalty situation as a coach, I try to win the game in the first round of 5 kicks. Therefore, I place my three best kickers in the following order and for the following reasons:

1. I would send my second best kicker first. He has practices and has confidence, and usually will convert.
2. I would send my fourth best kicker at this time because the chances of the first kicker scoring, and thereby reducing the pressure on the second kicker are very good.
3. My third best kicker will kick at this point since he has the confidence and composure to score even if the second player misses.
4. The worst kicker of the lot will take the fourth kick, because the third kicker probably scored and reduced the pressure.
5. My number one kicker will go fifth because many games are decided at this point. The team needs a good marksman with iron nerves.

While I agree that other coaches have successfully used other methods, my theory has yielded rich dividends for me over the years.

As a goalkeeper facing a penalty kick tiebreaker, I must devise a logical way of dealing with the situation. According to the strategy just described, I would assume that the best kickers (first, third and fifth) have practiced placing their kicks close to the uprights. Therefore, my strategy for these three players would be to determine, based on relevant clues, where they intend to place the ball, and dive into that corner as soon as they make contact.

The second and fourth kickers, not being as confident as the first, third and fifth kickers, might try to place the ball near the post and kick outside, be afraid of kicking outside and place the ball between the post and the goalkeeper, or kick the ball straight to the goalkeeper. They are the players most likely to err. Therefore my strategy as a goalkeeper would be to wait until the ball is kicked, try to determine as quickly as possible the path it is taking, and go after it, diving slightly forward to narrow the angle and maximize the chance of stopping the shot.

There will probably come a time when penalty kickers will become more sophisticated, making this theory obsolete. The important thing is that goalkeepers observe penalty kickers closely and devise their own theory. Stay with the theory for a while. Give it a chance to prove worthy or not. Be prepared to make adjustments if the theory backfires. As a goalkeeper I had to make many adjustments during the course of the playing season. For instance, I would arrive at a successful theory while representing

Figure 14-13

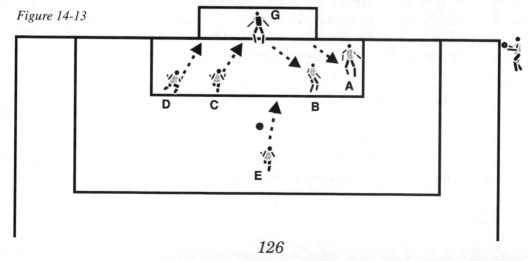

my country in international competition, only to find that it did not work when I competed in national league competition. Sometimes the theory adopted for international games might work with two or three of the top level clubs and fail with the less skilled clubs.

Although the theories you have devised for stopping penalty kicks may fail, the mere fact that you have a theory means that you have a positive attitude toward saving penalty kicks, which will maximize your chances of stopping these kicks.

Scoring Potential From Long Throws

Long throws in the attacking third of the field can produce many goalscoring opportunities for the offensive team. Goalkeepers must be aware of the vulnerable positions in front of the goal and the various options which are available to the attacking team. Let us look at long throw options that an attacking team might use in a game.

In Figure 14-13 two of the offensive team's most skillful headers, A and B, both attack the near post area. Player C attacks the space toward the middle of the goal, D attacks the space at the far post, and E is positioned around the penalty spot.

Figure 14-14 A illustrates the options which an attacking team may utilize on a long throw situation. The ball is thrown to A who has the option of heading (flick on) either to B at the near post, C at the middle of the goal, or D at the far post. If the service is on the penalty spot side of A, he has the option of heading the ball to E who is positioned at the penalty spot area. If the service is too low, A can play the ball back to the thrower.

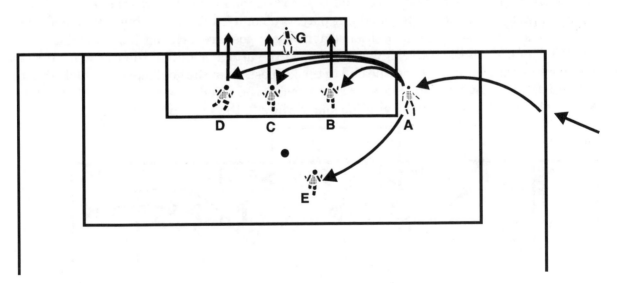

Figure 14-14A

In Figure 14-14B the long throw goes over the head of A. Attacker B, who is attacking the space behind A, is now in a good position to head on goal at the near post area. He also may elect to flick the ball on to C or D.

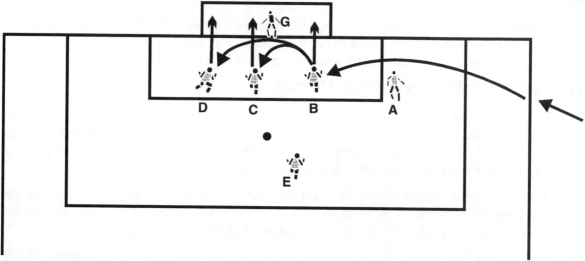

Figure 14-14B

Defending Against Long Throws

Defending against long throws is similar to defending against corner kicks. Two types of defensive alignments are commonly used: man-to-man and zone defense.

Man-to-Man Defense Against Long Throws

In Figure 14-15A two defenders (D^1 and D^2) are assigned to mark any space on the front and back post respectively. The remaining players all mark up an attacking player goalside and ballside. The goalkeeper is positioned at the near post area. He may have to adjust his position slightly based on the throwing range of the attacker taking the throw-in. If the thrower has the ability to throw the ball to the far post, then the goalkeeper should adjust his position by moving from the near post area to the middle part of the goal. At this position he can deal effectively with the long throws to the near and far post.

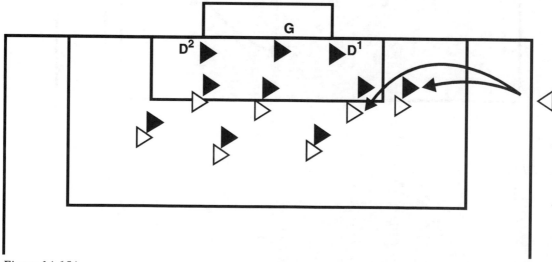

Figure 14-15A

Some attackers, despite being marked by taller players, are able to hold off their opponents long enough to consistently get their heads on the ball, thus creating dangerous situations in front of the goal. In a situation like this, I would position two defenders on that particular attacker (Fig. 14-15B). In the diagram defender D^1 marks attacker A from the rear. Defender D^3 marks him from the front. This tactic has worked successfully for me over the years both as a goalkeeper and a coach. I can remember vividly one important game when this tactic actually won the game for my team. I was the goalkeeper for my team, the Baltimore Comets, and the last game of the 1975 season was against the Dallas Tornado of the North American Soccer League. The winner of this game would secure a berth in the playoffs. In the first fifteen minutes of the game, Dallas squandered four goalscoring opportunities created by Kyle Rote Jr. from long throws. Kyle was unstoppable in the air, and it was just a matter of time before my team would concede a goal. As the goalkeeper I took the initiative in pulling back our team's 6-foot 3-inch center striker and positioned him in front of Kyle Rote Jr. This move paid off, because Kyle did not win another long throw for the remainder of the game and the Comets went on to win the game 2-1. This tactic threw Kyle off his game because he was unbeatable in the air only after taking a few preliminary steps forward before heading. With a defender in front of and behind him there was no place for him to go. The coach of our team did not make the change. As the goalkeeper I recognized the problem and solved it before we conceded a goal. It was difficult for the coach to make that change. Maybe he would have done it at the halftime but that might have been too late. Someone on the field had to take charge and make the appropriate adjustments to neutralize that dangerous attacking maneuver.

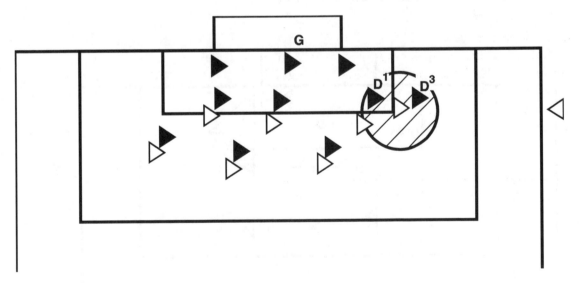

Figure 14-15B

Zone Defense Against Long Throws

The principles of the zone defense against long throws is similar to that of the zone defense for corner kicks. The players who are good headers of the ball are deployed in strategic positions in front of the goal. All other defending players are responsible for a particular area in front of the goal. Figure 14-16 illustrates a zone defense alignment which I use most commonly during long throw situations. The goalkeeper is positioned at the near post area. Defenders D^1, D^2, D^3 and D^4 are responsible for winning all throws to the near post area. Most teams have the tendency to throw the ball to the near post area for a tall attacker to flick to the far post. Therefore, the defenders deployed at the near post area must be the best headers of the ball on the team: D^2, D^3 and D^4 in that order. Defenders D^5 and D^6 both defend the middle part of the goal, while D^7, D^8, D^9 and D^{10} protect the back half of the goal should the long throw be flicked-on to the far post area. The goalkeeper is the key in foiling the long throw assault on his goal. He must feel free and comfortable in coming off his line to intercept the high balls. The deployment of defenders D^1, D^5, and D^{10} will assure the goalkeeper that his goal is well protected whenever he moves off his goal line to intercept a high ball.

The zone defense as illustrated in Figure 14-16 is just one approach to dealing with long throws. Other coaches have had success with zonal alignments that differ from the one presented in this chapter. There are several factors which determine where defenders should be positioned in a zone defense: the physical attributes of both attackers and defenders, the distance the thrower is capable of attaining on his long throws; the trajectory with which the ball is thrown — slow and in a straight line or with a high arch — and the width of the field.

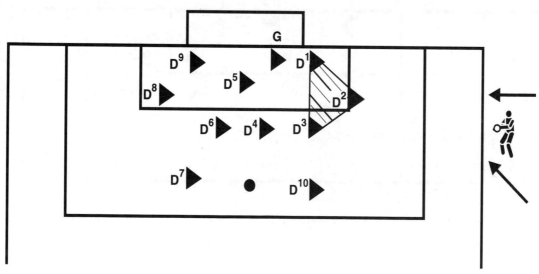

Figure 14-16

Chapter 15

The Psychological Dimension Of Goalkeeping

I t is obvious from the previous discussions how vital a quality goalkeeper is to the success of a team. He has massive responsibilities, physically, tactically, and psychologically. The game demands that the goalkeeper be responsible, confident in himself and his teammates, and able to favorably influence the outcome of a game as a result of his skills. The coach selecting a potential goalkeeper on the youth level, or deciding on his team's number one goalkeeper, therefore, wants to develop or select a leader who is not only technically competent but also able to instill confidence in his teammates.

To train goalkeepers effectively, coaches must make every effort to understand both the physical and mental demands of goalkeeping. Furthermore, they must include in the training regimen situations that will help develop and sharpen not only the goalkeeper's physical, technical, and tactical skills but also his psychological skills.

This chapter explores the psychological nuances of the goalkeeping position. It should help both players and coaches better understand that important aspect of the game.

It has been previously stated, and emphasized, that confidence and courage are the by-products of skill proficiency. Only after a player develops a high level of goalkeeping skill through long hours of intelligent hard work can he realistically enter a game with the self-confidence necessary to deal effectively with the various demands of the position.

Psychological Concerns During Training

The goalkeeper's attitude toward training must be positive. He must always come to practice with one objective in mind: to become a better goalkeeper. The ability to set realistic goals for every practice session, and the discipline to work conscientiously to achieve them, develops yet another important mental skill; concentration.

Building Confidence Between Goalkeeper And Players

The goalkeeper who is to play a major role in directing the course of the game must understand completely both his role and that of his teammates, especially the defenders. In training sessions, the coach must provide the goalkeeper with opportunities to work with and direct his teammates, not stick him in a corner to do drills the entire session. This is the only way to improve communication between goalkeepers and their teammates. The goalkeeper can also seize opportunities before and after practice to clarify any misunderstandings between himself and his defenders.

The coach's attitude toward goalkeeping must also be positive. He must treat the goalkeeper with respect. The goalkeeper needs to be involved in tactical defensive situations and discussing possible tactical solutions. The position of goalkeeping should be treated as a very important part of the training session, not just as a chance to provide shooting practice for the outfield players. During shooting practice the same amount of coaching afforded an outfield player who shoots the ball too high should also be made available to the goalkeeper if he fails to gather the ball cleanly on a dive.

During shooting practice, the coach must also demonstrate concern for the goalkeeper's safety. Very often coaches, in their zeal to expose outside players to shooting situations in front of the goal, neglect the safety of the goalkeeper. For instance many practice fields have very hard and uneven areas in front of the goals, some of them littered with stones making it painful or even dangerous for the goalkeeper to dive. The coach should recognize such unsafe conditions and either ensure that the goalkeeper is dressed adequately for the conditions (in knee and elbow pads, padded shorts or long pants, etc.), move the goal to a grassy area (if it is portable), or use the area behind the goal, which is usually very grassy or less uneven than that in front. Realizing that his coach is thinking of his welfare and treats him the same way he treats the other players (in terms of equality and quality of work in practice sessions and coaching attention) enhances the goalkeeper's whole attitude regarding his self-worth and the value of his position. Failure to treat the goalkeeper as an integral part of the team serves only to affect his mental attitude, eroding confidence, commitment, and self-worth.

Psychological Concerns on Game Day

Although a goalkeeper may be skilled in every aspect of goalkeeping, there are many circumstances which can cause him to lose confidence in himself on game days. A few examples follow:

Pre-Game

This is the period when the player packs his equipment bag in preparation for the game. If he forgets any of the items listed below he is liable to feel very uncomfortable — uncomfortable enough to throw him completely off his game:

- Gloves
- An alternate color jersey in case of color conflict (see Chapter 10)
- Extra shoes, plus accessories (extra studs and instruments to replace them)

During this time, the goalkeeper must (a) allow himself adequate time to prepare for the game physically and mentally — if he needs an extensive tape job he must arrive in the dressing room early enough to allow all taping to be completed in time for him to warm-up adequately; (b) ensure that equipment and uniform are fitted properly at least 30 minutes prior to kickoff; (c) make sure that all necessary alternate equipment and accessories are in one bag and available at a moment's notice (during the game). For instance, in muddy conditions, the goalkeeper's gloves might lose traction causing him to drop balls, (and lose confidence). A prepared goalkeeper would have an extra pair of gloves in his bag inside the goal ready to make a switch if it becomes necessary.

Warm-Ups on the Field

Coaches must avoid warm-up drills or any situation where there is a potential for many goals to be scored on the goalkeeper during this period. Having the forwards score frequently in warm-ups increases their confidence but might destroy the goalkeeper's. Unless, of course, the goalkeeper relishes that opportunity to display his gymnastic ability in order to psyche out any opponents who are looking on. Before choosing warm-up methods, the coach should make sure to understand the psychological makeup of the goalkeeper and select activities that will develop, not destroy, his confidence.

Start of Game

The sooner the goalkeeper touches the ball, the better it is for his confidence. This point cannot be overemphasized. My personal experience provides a good example.

In 1976 I was playing for the NASL's Baltimore Comets against the Boston Minutemen. The field was wet and for the first time an Adidas (Tango) ball was used (instead of the customary Mitre ball). The Adidas ball was manufactured with a waterproof plastic coating to ensure that it kept its weight in wet conditions, but which also made the ball very difficult to handle (slippery). About ten minutes elapsed before I got my first touch of the ball (by way of a high cross from the left side). To my amazement, the ball slipped through my hands. Luckily my fullback headed the ball off the line. This early shock affected my confidence and concentration adversely for the balance of the game.

Goalkeepers must familiarize themselves with (1) the type of ball, (2) ground conditions, (3) size of field, and (4) the position of the sun or lights.

During the Game

Goalkeepers should make a point of saving shots cleanly to avoid making saves look more difficult than they really are. If the goalkeeper starts dropping balls, diving unnecessarily, and punching away air balls that should be caught, the opposing attackers might assume that the goalkeeper is nervous or incompetent, and thereby gain confidence and seize every opportunity to shoot. The defenders, sensing that their goalkeeper is a bit shaky, might become unsettled themselves and may not be able to perform at their normal level.

Conversely, if the goalkeeper handles shots on goal cleanly and deals with the most difficult shots as though they did not challenge him in the least, the defenders will gain confidence and might be inspired to play well above themselves, while the attackers might be discouraged from shooting.

If a goalkeeper makes a technical or tactical error in a game, coaches and teammates should avoid taking him to task. Instead they should offer support (or say nothing) to bolster his confidence. Coaches and outside players should familiarize themselves with the way a goalkeeper feels when a goal is scored on him. Yes, that is the way a goalkeeper and everyone else views a goal scoring situation, as a goal being scored against the goalkeeper, or the goalkeeper giving up a goal, not as a goal scored against the team, or as the team collectively giving up a goal. The blame ultimately falls on the person between the uprights: the goalkeeper. This is a very heavy burden for one player to carry.

Allow me to share what goes on in a goalkeeper's mind when a goal is scored, and how coaches and teammates could lessen his mental anguish. To a goalkeeper, the sound of the ball making contact with the net ("net music" as I used to call it) is one of the most demoralizing sounds in the whole world. There you are, sprawled on the ground, hearing the goal perhaps before you even see it go in, looking back to see the ball lodged in the corner of the net. Then finally to see all ten of your teammates with hands on their waist or heads with expressions on their faces as if to say "how could you let us down?" At this point the poor goalkeeper wants to die.

The next demoralizing event is the degrading trip to the back of the net to retrieve the ball, especially if it is in the far, deep corner of the net. At this point, the one thing the goalkeeper doesn't need is criticism — from players or coaches.

I was very fortunate that I always had a good working relationship with my defenders. I always encouraged my defenders, even when they made goal scoring mistakes. Because of my positive attitude during tense moments, my defenders also returned the same type of support to me when it was necessary. The result — a very positive and supportive defense working hard and utilizing every ounce of their physical and mental resources to prevent a goal from scoring. Two defenders come to mind as being the two most supportive players I have ever played with: Victor Gamaldo and Tyrone DeLabasitde. We played together for more than 15 years on high school, World Cup and professional levels. Whenever I gave up a goal, I would hear Victor and Tyrone saying to the other defenders, "Lincoln is having a bad day, let's keep it real tight." This positive behavior of my teammates did not occur automatically. They responded with the same sensitivity and positiveness that I offered to them over the years.

When A Goal is Scored

Coaches and players must understand that the moment a goal is scored is crucial to any team's success or failure. Let us analyze this situation (when a goal is scored) carefully and try to recognize the attitudes that contribute to the success and/or failure of teams during this critical period. Sometimes we have seen or played games where the teams are matched equally. The rhythm of play and score attest to the equal strength of the two teams. The score is deadlocked at 0-0. Then, suddenly, the goalkeeper commits a cardinal sin — he takes his eyes off the ball, and it slips through his hands for a goal. At this point the thought of the game being lost is a realistic conclusion, especially if in previous encounters the games were always decided by one goal. Tempers are flaring, defenders are screaming at the goalkeeper. The goalkeeper is on his knees holding his head, while the other players hang their heads down dejectedly, and the ball remains at the back of the net for the longest while. At this point, the team is mentally down and vulnerable.

The opponents, on the other hand, are all fired up and at last have that sweet taste of victory. As the ball is kicked off, the team that has just scored the goal regains possession, through either a careless pass made by a dejected opponent or the aggressive play of a fired up teammate. They score again in less than five minutes, and follow up with another goal in as many minutes.

The question is, how can a game be won by so many goals when the teams are of equal strength? There is, of course, no simple answer. However, the key issue here is that when the first goal is scored, the players on the losing team may have lost their composure by arguing with the goalkeeper, therefore leaving themselves vulnerable, albeit for only a short period. The initiative must come from somewhere to be supportive and determined to prevent another goal, and in fact, immediately seek the equalizer. The goalkeeper can play a key role in providing support to his teammates by quickly retrieving the ball from the goal and kicking it back to the center of the field and shouting enthusiastically "Come on guys, let's go, keep your heads up, one goal can't beat our team." The coach also must understand that the groundwork for such tenacity and spirit is laid in quality practice. Develop competent skills and positive methods of dealing with adversity so that the goalkeeper's and the team's confidence can weather these critical moments successfully.

Every situation should be considered a ground for learning and growth. The coach must be sensitive to this and turn what appears to be negative development into a positive learning experience. The challenge for the goalkeeper and the coach is to continue to expand this ability so that decisions may be made more rapidly in supportive context.

Conclusion

After many years of playing and teaching the game of soccer, the one truth I have learned is, "The more you think you know about the game, the less you know."

The beauty of soccer is that it allows everyone to meet its demands at whatever level he plays. This book is intended as an introduction for the coach, player or the interested fan.

It was written with the idea of sharing practical techniques, approaches, and understanding of the goalkeeper's position from the goalkeeper's point of view. To be useful it will have to be read and reread. There are no magical formulas to transform a poor goalkeeper into a quality goalkeeper overnight. The formulas presented in this book require intensive training, patience, discipline, and good work ethics if they are to help a player achieve quality goalkeeper status.

As I reflect, and reread chapters of this book, I cannot help but want to change a word here or a word there because the essence of the position is "sense, touch, and instinct." Even ideal circumstances are difficult to explain, since they change from day to day.

I would hope that coaches, upon reviewing this work, will appreciate the importance and difficulty of the position of goalkeeper and allocate quality time during practice sessions to reinforce the goalkeeper's technical, tactical and mental roles.

For the player I would hope that this book has stimulated thought on how to adapt and meet the requirements of the goalkeeping position. I am not of the school that says you must become bloody and bowed throwing yourself about the pitch to master the techniques of play. I prefer to think that the position requires introspection, practice, dedication, and belief in oneself as the foundation for excellent performance.

While growing up, I was not the most gifted and graceful athlete. In fact, I was always the youngster who was "put in goal" because I was not as old or as good as my peers on the pitch. However, as the years went by and my ability improved, I became more than the extra man. In retrospect, I need to thank the players for giving me part of that incentive and to recognize that those early morning sessions with the goalkeeper sages of Trinidad helped me shape and form my understanding of the position.

This book has forced me to think through many issues and nuances of playing the position of goalkeeper, and the game itself. I hope it has been helpful and I also hope it stimulates you, the reader, to come to the conclusion that I did...to start the unfinished chapters. It's still KEEPER'S BALL!

Glossary

Angle, narrowing the: applied to the goalkeeper who has moved closer to the ball in order to reduce the shooting space on goal.

Angle, diving: the angle at which the goalkeeper dives in relation to the ball and the goal.

Anchorman: the defensive player who is responsible for lining himself up with the ball and the near post in a defensive wall, during free kick situations.

Blind side: defensively speaking, the side opposite the ball.

Communication: to convey ideas through speech or signal, e.g. the goalkeeper shouts "Keeper!" in a high cross situation signaling to his defenders that he is moving off his line to intercept the cross.

Corner kick: a kick awarded when the ball travels over the goal line and is last played by a defender.

Corner, conventional: long (direct) corner kicks.

Corner, short: an indirect corner kick situation in which the kicker makes a short pass to a teammate who crosses the ball or takes a shot on goal.

Cross: a pass origination from the flanks across the face of the goal, on the ground or in the air.

Cross, high or lofted: an aerial cross from the flanks across the face of the goal.

Cushion: the withdrawal of the hands or body upon contact with the ball to absorb the impact of a shot.

Defenders: all players on the team that is not in possession of the ball. However, the word defender usually implies the last line of players whose primary responsibility is to prevent goals from scoring.

Defense: usually implies the last line of defenders in front of the goalkeeper.

Defense, space behind the: the area between the goalkeeper and the last defender(s).

Distribution: kicking or throwing the ball to an outfield teammate.

Far post: the upright that is farthest away from the shooter.

Fake or feint: a deceptive movement with or without the ball, such as in a one-on-one situation where the goalkeeper feints or fakes to dive to his left but goes to the right instead.

Flight: refers to the trajectory of a shot or pass.

Flight, behind or in line with the: moving the body or hands behind the trajectory of the ball.

Free kick, direct: a kick awarded to the opposing team as a penalty for committing any of ten specified penal offenses (see penal offenses). A goal can be scored directly from a direct free kick.

Free kick, indirect: awarded after commission of any infringement that is not a penal offense. A goal cannot be scored directly from an indirect free kick. The ball must come in contact with a second player (any player, teammate or opponent) before the goal is allowed.

Ground shy: fearful of making contact with the ground usually as a result of an injury sustained while diving in a game or practice.

Instep: the top part of the foot, the lace of the shoe.

Jugs: the brand name of a device that ejects balls (soccer, tennis, baseball) by way of two rotating wheels.

Mark: guarding an opponent with the intent of denying him the ball.

Marking, man-to-man: defensive play based upon guarding an individual opponent rather than an area of the field.

Offside: a player is offside if he has fewer than two defenders between himself and the goal line and is nearer to the goal line than the ball at the precise moment the ball is played (unless if he receives the ball directly from a drop ball, a corner kick, a throw in or if he is in his own half of the field).

Offside trap: a planned defensive maneuver by the rearmost defender(s) to deliberately place the attacking team's player(s) in an offside position.

Penal offenses: fouls and misconduct punishable by a direct free kick. The ten penal offenses are: handling the ball, striking or attempting to strike an opponent, pushing (with the hands), holding, tripping, kicking or attempting to kick an opponent, tackling in a violent manner, pushing (with the body), charging in a violent manner and spitting at an opponent. Should a penal offense occur in the penalty are, a penalty kick would be awarded.

Playing big: a goalkeeper who reduces an attacker's shooting space on goal by narrowing the angle and staying on his feet as long as possible is referred to as "playing big."

Ready stance: the goalkeeper's stance prior to a shot, e.g. feet comfortable apart and parallel to each other, weight on balls of the feet, knees slightly bent, etc.

Rhythm, shooting: the sequence of movements made by the goalkeeper in response to an attacker's shooting rhythm.

Rhythm, goalkeeping: the sequence of movements made by the goalkeeper in response to an attacker's shooting rhythm.

Shoot-outs: a method of deciding the winner of a tied game using a specified number of penalty kicks awarded to each team. The team scoring the most penalty kicks wins the game.

Sweeper: a space-marking defender positioned behind a line of two or more man-marking defenders.

Space kick: kick made across the face of the ball with the outside of the instep.

Stay home: refers to a goalkeeper's decision to stay in his goal area instead of moving out to intercept a cross or through pass.

Timing, goalkeeping: the ability to know the precise moment an attacker is about to take a shot. Proper timing is absolutely vital in initiating goalkeeping rhythm.

Untidiness: fumbling or dropping the ball after a shot on goal.

Volley: kicking the ball with the instep before it makes contact with the ground.

Volley, half: kicking the ball with the top of the instep immediately after the ball makes contact with the ground.

About the Author

L incoln Phillips has enjoyed great success as a player and coach on youth, college and professional levels. A native of Trinidad & Tobago, Lincoln led his high school team (Queen's Royal College) and club teams (Providence F.C., Maple F. C., and The Trinidad & Tobago Regiment) to several league and national championships. Considered the leading goalkeeper in the West Indies, he led the Trinidad & Tobago national team to a bronze medal in the Pan American Games in 1967. Dubbed "El Tigre" (The Tiger) by his fans for his stealth and acrobatic style of goalkeeping, he received numerous individual honors including: player of the year, and captain of the year, and held a long standing shutout record of 20 consecutive scoreless games in 1962.

Lincoln soon caught the eyes of North American Soccer League talent scouts and was recruited by the Baltimore Bays in 1968. At the end of the season he was named player/coach of the Washington Darts of the American Soccer League. He led the Darts to two ASL championships in 1968 &1969 and to the North American Soccer League in 1970. Lincoln was also named to the ASL all-star team in 1968 & 1969 and to the NASL all-star team (1970) as a player and coach in a game against Santos of Brazil. At the end of the 1970 NASL season several records were established, three of which were set by Lincoln and remained intact for more than ten years: the most consecutive wins in one season, for a coach; the longest consecutive shutout streak and the largest number of shutouts in one season (*Guinness Book of Records*, 1970-80).

In the fall of 1970, Lincoln Phillips shifted gears from the pros to the college ranks and continued his winning ways leading Howard University to a National Collegiate Athletic Association Division 1 Championship in 1974. Lincoln earned his Bachelor's and Master of Science Degrees in physical education while coaching at Howard University. He published several articles for physical education journals and sports magazines including: *Cinematographic Analysis of Soccer Goalkeeping Techniques*, 1979 (Master of Science Thesis), *Young Athlete Magazine*: "So You Want To Be A Goalkeeper?," and Crawford, Phillips and Moultree: "Exertional Bradycardia Compensation To Orthostasis." From 1984 to 1987 Lincoln served as Director of Physical Education and Athletics at the Town & Country/Newport Preparatory School.

Lincoln is a certified United States Soccer Federation "A" License coach and is currently a staff member of the USSF National Coaching Schools. He has most recently been added to the FIFA (Federation of International Football Association) board of coaches. He has also been inducted in the Howard University Hall of Fame and the Trinidad and Tobago Hall of Fame. Lincoln has been instrumental in spreading the soccer word to coaches throughout the United States as the current Director of Coaching for Seneca Soccer Association and former Director of Coaching for the Maryland State Youth Soccer Association and the Soccer Association of Columbia. As President of the Lincoln Phillips Soccer School, Inc., Lincoln has touched the lives of thousands of boys and girls (ages 5-18) who attended and benefited from LPSS' philosophy and commitment to setting standards that better the students' character and improve their appreciation of and skill in soccer.